T0209672

An Analysis of

Immanuel Kant's

Critique of Pure Reason

Michael O'Sullivan

Published by Macat International Ltd
24:13 Coda Centre, 189 Munster Road, London SW6 6AW.

Distributed exclusively by Routledge
2 Park Square, Milton Park, Abingdon, Oxon OX14 4RN
711 Third Avenue, New York, NY 10017, USA

Routledge is an imprint of the Taylor & Francis Group, an informa business

www.macat.com
info@macat.com

Cataloguing in Publication Data
A catalogue record for this book is available from the British Library.
Library of Congress Cataloguing-in-Publication Data is available upon request.
Cover illustration: Etienne Gilfillan

ISBN 978-1-912303-03-8 (hardback)
ISBN 978-1-912127-70-2 (paperback)
ISBN 978-1-912281-91-6 (e-book)

Notice
The information in this book is designed to orientate readers of the work under analysis,
to elucidate and contextualise its key ideas and themes, and to aid in the development
of critical thinking skills. It is not meant to be used, nor should it be used, as a
substitute for original thinking or in place of original writing or research. References and
notes are provided for informational purposes and their presence does not constitute
endorsement of the information or opinions therein. This book is presented solely for
educational purposes. It is sold on the understanding that the publisher is not engaged
to provide any scholarly advice. The publisher has made every effort to ensure that
this book is accurate and up-to-date, but makes no warranties or representations with
regard to the completeness or reliability of the information it contains. The information
and the opinions provided herein are not guaranteed or warranted to produce particular
results and may not be suitable for students of every ability. The publisher shall not be
liable for any loss, damage or disruption arising from any errors or omissions, or from
the use of this book, including, but not limited to, special, incidental, consequential or
other damages caused, or alleged to have been caused, directly or indirectly, by the
information contained within.

CONTENTS

THE MACAT LIBRARY

The Macat Library is a series of unique academic explorations of seminal works in the humanities and social sciences – books and papers that have had a significant and widely recognised impact on their disciplines. It has been created to serve as much more than just a summary of what lies between the covers of a great book. It illuminates and explores the influences on, ideas of, and impact of that book. Our goal is to offer a learning resource that encourages critical thinking and fosters a better, deeper understanding of important ideas.

Each publication is divided into three Sections: Influences, Ideas, and Impact. Each Section has four Modules. These explore every important facet of the work, and the responses to it.

This Section-Module structure makes a Macat Library book easy to use, but it has another important feature. Because each Macat book is written to the same format, it is possible (and encouraged!) to cross-reference multiple Macat books along the same lines of inquiry or research. This allows the reader to open up interesting interdisciplinary pathways.

To further aid your reading, lists of glossary terms and people mentioned are included at the end of this book (these are indicated by an asterisk [*] throughout) – as well as a list of works cited.

Macat has worked with the University of Cambridge to identify the elements of critical thinking and understand the ways in which six different skills combine to enable effective thinking.
Three allow us to fully understand a problem; three more give us the tools to solve it. Together, these six skills make up the **PACIER** model of critical thinking. They are:

ANALYSIS – understanding how an argument is built
EVALUATION – exploring the strengths and weaknesses of an argument
INTERPRETATION – understanding issues of meaning

CREATIVE THINKING – coming up with new ideas and fresh connections
PROBLEM-SOLVING – producing strong solutions
REASONING – creating strong arguments

To find out more, visit **WWW.MACAT.COM.**

CRITICAL THINKING AND *CRITIQUE OF PURE REASON*

Primary critical thinking skill: CREATIVE THINKING
Secondary critical thinking skill: EVALUATION

Immanuel Kant's *Critique of Pure Reason* is one of the most influential works in the history of philosophy – not to mention one of the most challenging. Its topic is the nature of human knowledge, and the question of whether or not it is possible to have knowledge of the world at all.

Over two centuries later, Kant's treatise remains a subject of fierce debate among philosophers, who continue to offer new interpretations of his meaning. What is not in doubt is the work's originality and brilliance – nor its mastery of creative thinking.

Creative thinkers are able to bring a new perspective to questions and problems, look at things from a different angle, and show them in a fresh light. Kant achieved this by mediating between the two major schools of philosophical thought concerning knowledge – empiricism and rationalism – to create a complex third way. Where empiricists believed all knowledge is founded on experience, and rationalists believed true knowledge is founded on reason alone, Kant evaluated their arguments and proposed a third position – one incorporating elements of both, but within specific limits. As infamously dense at is profound, Kant's *Critique* shows creative thinking operating at a level few can aspire to reach.

ABOUT THE AUTHOR OF THE ORIGINAL WORK

Immanuel Kant, the man who changed the way the world thinks about thoughts, lived a singularly uneventful life. Born in 1724 in the Prussian city of Königsberg (now Kaliningrad, Russia), Kant rarely left his hometown. He taught at the local university and wrote. He never married, and died in Königsberg in 1804. But his many insightful philosophical works brought him widespread fame in his lifetime, and he continues to be regarded as one of the world's greatest philosophers

ABOUT THE AUTHOR OF THE ANALYSIS

Dr Michael O'Sullivan is a tutor in the Department of Philosophy, King's College London. He is the editor of *Wittgenstein and Perception*.

ABOUT MACAT

GREAT WORKS FOR CRITICAL THINKING

Macat is focused on making the ideas of the world's great thinkers accessible and comprehensible to everybody, everywhere, in ways that promote the development of enhanced critical thinking skills.

It works with leading academics from the world's top universities to produce new analyses that focus on the ideas and the impact of the most influential works ever written across a wide variety of academic disciplines. Each of the works that sit at the heart of its growing library is an enduring example of great thinking. But by setting them in context – and looking at the influences that shaped their authors, as well as the responses they provoked – Macat encourages readers to look at these classics and game-changers with fresh eyes. Readers learn to think, engage and challenge their ideas, rather than simply accepting them.

'Macat offers an amazing first-of-its-kind tool for interdisciplinary learning and research. Its focus on works that transformed their disciplines and its rigorous approach, drawing on the world's leading experts and educational institutions, opens up a world-class education to anyone.'

Andreas Schleicher
Director for Education and Skills, Organisation for Economic Co-operation and Development

'Macat is taking on some of the major challenges in university education ... They have drawn together a strong team of active academics who are producing teaching materials that are novel in the breadth of their approach.'

Prof Lord Broers,
former Vice-Chancellor of the University of Cambridge

'The Macat vision is exceptionally exciting. It focuses upon new modes of learning which analyse and explain seminal texts which have profoundly influenced world thinking and so social and economic development. It promotes the kind of critical thinking which is essential for any society and economy. This is the learning of the future.'

Rt Hon Charles Clarke, former UK Secretary of State for Education

'The Macat analyses provide immediate access to the critical conversation surrounding the books that have shaped their respective discipline, which will make them an invaluable resource to all of those, students and teachers, working in the field.'

Professor William Tronzo, University of California at San Diego

WAYS IN TO THE TEXT

KEY POINTS

- Immanuel Kant (1724–1804) was a Prussian philosopher who shaped the course of modern Western philosophy.

- *Critique of Pure Reason* claims to end previous disputes in metaphysics* — the study of the ultimate nature of reality or being — and explain the possibility of human knowledge.

- Kant urged that philosophers investigate the very possibility of human knowledge.

Who was Immanuel Kant?

Born in the East Prussian* city of Königsberg (now Kaliningrad, Russia) in 1724, Immanuel Kant rarely left his hometown. He never married, and spent his life as a scholar, rising to the position of professor at the University of Königsberg. An expert on philosophy, he also taught and wrote about astronomy, physics, geography, and other topics.

Kant published the *Critique of Pure Reason* in 1781, at the age of 57. A highly original work of philosophy, the *Critique* presented the foundations of a new philosophical system. Kant spent the rest of his life developing it. His most important later works were the *Critique of Practical Reason* and the *Critique of Judgment*. Together, the three books present Kant's "critical" philosophy.

Other scholars quickly recognized the *Critique* as a revolutionary achievement, bringing Kant widespread fame.

Kant died in 1804, but he continues to be regarded as one of the greatest philosophers who ever lived. His work has had an enormous influence on later philosophers, whether they developed his ideas or reacted against them.

What Does *Pure Reason* Say?

Kant asks, "How is it possible to know anything about the world?" In his view, two things are necessary for knowledge: intuitions and concepts. Roughly, intuitions are perceptual experiences. Concepts are the general categories in terms of which we understand things. Humans need both intuitions and concepts to perceive things and to think about them.

But Kant thinks we know certain things *a priori*,* a Latin phrase literally meaning "from the previous." We do not learn *a priori* things from experience; we know them independently. One example is our knowledge of causality: we know certain things in nature cause each other. But not, Kant thinks, because we see things that way.

Still, if Kant's thesis is true—if knowledge requires both intuitions and concepts—how is *a priori* knowledge possible?

Kant believes we have *a priori* knowledge only of appearances, not of things as they are in themselves. This answer is part of what he calls his "Copernican revolution." The fifteenth-century astronomer Copernicus* showed that the Earth travels around the Sun, upending the long-standing belief that the Sun orbited the Earth. Kant's similarly revolutionary thesis shows that we have knowledge of causality not because of the structure of the world but because of the structure of our minds. We cannot help but interpret things as causing each other. Things in themselves are not causal. They appear that way to us. Kant believed that other sorts of *a priori* knowledge functioned in the same way.

Kant also discusses metaphysics.* Traditionally, metaphysics addresses such things as God, the soul, and the question of whether life after death exists. Despite discussing these issues for thousands of years—and in contrast with the progress science had made in explaining the natural world—metaphysicians had still not managed to resolve them. Metaphysicians in Kant's day possessed no more knowledge about the discipline than the ancient Greeks had.

The problem, Kant explains, is that metaphysics attempts to know what cannot be known. Humans cannot have perceptual experiences of God, the soul, or a future life. We can use our concepts to discuss these things, but have no intuitions to apply them to. Kant theorized that knowledge requires both intuitions and concepts, so metaphysical topics remain beyond all possible human knowledge.

Still, Kant recognizes that we cannot simply stop discussing metaphysical concepts, because they are part of our natural curiosity as human beings. Questions about God and the soul arise naturally and we should not try to ignore them but we must recognize that we can never arrive at definitive answers to these questions.

Kant's argument causes us to move inward, to see how knowledge depends on both our minds and the outside world. His philosophy has made important contributions both to how we understand scientific knowledge of the natural world, and to how we understand whether we can have any knowledge beyond the natural world.

Why Does *Pure Reason* Matter?

Many class *Critique of Pure Reason* as one of the greatest philosophical books of all time. Arguably the most important philosophical work of the last few centuries, it has influenced generations of philosophers from all over the world, working in many different philosophical traditions.

It is also a demanding and difficult work, with a long, complicated argument. The language is also challenging. Kant introduces many new and strange terms the reader must learn in order to understand the argument.

Still, *Critique* remains an essential work of philosophy for several reasons. First, it remains relevant to many different topics. Kant touches on mathematics, science, psychology, theology, and other disciplines. In each case, he puts forward influential views about the possibility of human knowledge. Anyone interested in the philosophy of mathematics, or the philosophy of religion, for example, must understand Kant's approach.

Critique introduced a revolutionary argument that changed the way philosophers viewed their subject. Before Kant, philosophers focused on understanding the structure of the world. Kant urged us to focus on understanding the structure of the human mind. That, he believed, would help us see what human beings can and cannot know.

This is what Kant called the "critical" attitude: reflecting on the limitations of knowledge and thought. Today it's accepted as a general technique for thinking about difficult questions. We do not just ask what the answer is, but also whether it is the kind of question human beings can answer. Modern philosophers have extended the idea to include the limitations of what language can express.

SECTION 1
INFLUENCES

MODULE 1
THE AUTHOR AND THE HISTORICAL CONTEXT

KEY POINTS

- Kant's *Critique* continues to influence philosophers today.

- Kant was exposed to the major early modern philosophical schools of rationalism* and empiricism.*

- Kant regarded his work as a philosophical expression of the values of the Enlightenment,* the cultural and intellectual movement of seventeenth- and eighteenth-century Europe and North America.

Why Read this Text?

Immanuel Kant's *Critique of Pure Reason* may be the most significant work of modern Western philosophy. With this book, Kant claimed to have brought about a revolution in philosophy equivalent to that of the fifteenth-century astronomer Copernicus,* who argued that the Earth orbits the Sun and not the other way round.[1] One of Kant's key concepts was that before we can ponder the nature of the world we must first ponder our minds. He set out various intellectual tools for doing just that. In the more than two hundred years since Kant published this work, every philosopher has had to respond to this notion, whether they agree or disagree with it.

In the preface, Kant describes the current state of metaphysics*— the study of the ultimate nature of reality or being— as a "battlefield" on which "endless controversies" have been fought.[2] Kant regards these battles as fruitless. The *Critique* does not take sides in these disputes. Rather, it attempts to bypass the battlefield altogether. By using reason to investigate the grounds and scope of his claims, Kant

> ❝ *Enlightenment* is man's emergence from his self-incurred immaturity. *Immaturity* is the inability to use one's own understanding without the guidance of another. This immaturity is *self-incurred* if its cause is not lack of understanding, but lack of resolution and courage to use it without the guidance of another. The motto of enlightenment is therefore: *Sapere aude* [dare to know]! Have courage to use your own understanding. ❞
>
> Immanuel Kant, *An Answer to the Question "What is Enlightenment?"*

hopes to end these controversies. By exposing the intellectual roots of philosophers' temptation to indulge in free-floating metaphysical speculation, the *Critique* also seeks to help potential philosophical combatants stay clear of the battlefield as well.

Today, few philosophers accept all of Kant's central arguments. Given *Critique*'s extraordinary ambition and range, this should not be surprising. Nevertheless, a vast number of Kant's arguments and theories continue to find defenders and followers. In contending that we should replace metaphysical thought with an enquiry into the conditions of metaphysical thought itself, Kant remains highly influential.

Author's Life

Born in 1724, Kant was brought up in Königsberg, the capital of East Prussia* (today, the Russian city of Kaliningrad). While not a major intellectual and artistic center, Königsberg was hardly the irrelevant backwater traditionally depicted in accounts of Kant's life,[3] An important legal, military, and economic area, it also boasted a significant university.

Kant's family made harnesses. They brought him up in the Pietistic* form of Protestantism, which emphasized morality over religious doctrine. The schooling he received at the local Collegium Fredericianum followed the same tradition. When he was 16, Kant enrolled in Königsberg University. He aspired to teach there, and in 1770, achieved the rank of professor of logic and metaphysics.

Kant published the first edition of his *Critique* in 1781; a second, revised, edition followed in 1787. In a letter to philosopher Moses Mendelssohn,* he claimed that although he had been working on *Critique*'s ideas and arguments for around 12 years, he actually wrote the work in just four to five months.[4] Scholars generally find this claim unlikely.[5]

Kant never married, and is said to have led a very scholarly lifestyle, marked by routine. He rarely, if ever, left Königsberg, and died there in 1804.

Author's Background

A rather rarefied and abstract work of metaphysics and epistemology,*—the philosophical study of the nature of knowledge and of the justification of belief—*Critique* was not directly influenced by specific social and political circumstances. Nor did it respond to any. However, scholars generally regard the work as a defining product of the late Enlightenment, the eighteenth-century movement that promoted the use of reason. This assessment is only partially accurate.

True, *Critique* conforms to the general spirit of the Enlightenment, as Kant identifies human reason as the main way of discovering truths. On the other hand, it argues that reason has limited applications.

While Kant aimed *Critique* primarily at academic philosophers, he would also have had the philosophically educated public in mind. This reflected a widespread aspect of the Enlightenment. In Germany, "popular philosophers" saw themselves as spreading the word of the Enlightenment. Like the French *philosophes** whose works they translated and admired, these people wanted philosophy to reach beyond the university and to affect public political and religious life.

This may sound like a revolutionary idea, but the popular philosophers were hardly revolutionaries in the political sense. They primarily aimed to combat superstition and spread scientific knowledge.[6] Kant sympathized with this outlook, although he certainly did not write *Critique* in a way that would be easily accessible to the contemporary German public.

NOTES

1   Immanuel Kant, *Critique of Pure Reason*, trans. Paul Guyer and Allen W. Wood (Cambridge: Cambridge University Press, 1998), Bxvi.

2   Kant, *Critique of Pure Reason*, Aviii.

3   For a survey of early biographical materials on Kant, see Manfred Kuehn, *Kant: A Biography* (Cambridge: Cambridge University Press, 2001), 1–24.

4   Immanuel Kant, *Correspondence*, trans. and ed. Arnulf Zweig (Cambridge: Cambridge University Press, 1999), 190.

5   Kuehn, *Kant: A Biography*, 241.

6   See Frederick C. Beiser, *The Fate of Reason: German Philosophy from Kant to Fichte* (Cambridge, MA: Harvard University Press, 1987), 165–9.

MODULE 2
ACADEMIC CONTEXT

KEY POINTS

- Philosophy investigates the nature and meaning both of reality and of our *knowledge* of reality.

- Following sixteenth-century French philosopher René Descartes,* modern philosophy in Kant's day focused on the nature and justification of our claims to knowledge.

- Kant argued that philosophy had neglected the critical question of how we can have thoughts about reality at all.

The Work In Its Context

Immanuel Kant's *Critique of Pure Reason* reflects several preoccupations of European philosophy in his day. For example, the philosophical discipline of epistemology*— the study of what we can know and how we can attain knowledge—lies at the center of the work. Kant's *Critique* stands at least partly in the tradition of sixteenth-century French philosopher René Descartes. Descartes, generally considered the father of modern philosophy, gave the discipline an epistemological focus. *Critique* also discusses concepts common to philosophy that came after Descartes (called post-Cartesian* philosophy), such as causality and substance.* The nature of substance was a common and controversial theme in early modern philosophy. Generally speaking, it is that in which the properties of an object inhere, or become fixed.

While the topics may not be new, Kant treats them in intriguing new ways. Not content just to find new answers to puzzles generations of philosophers had struggled with, Kant's new method of philosophy does not attack metaphysical problems directly. He changes the nature of the puzzles by subtly shifting the direction in which he looks for an

> **❝** [Reason] thereby falls into obscurity and contradictions, from which it can indeed surmise that it must somewhere be proceeding on the ground of hidden errors; but it cannot discover them, for the principles on which it is proceeding, since they surpass the bounds of all experience, no longer recognize any touchstone of experience. The battlefield of these endless controversies is called metaphysics. **❞**
> Immanuel Kant, *Critique of Pure Reason*

answer. Kant's shift in philosophical focus is, in part, what made *Critique* so difficult for his contemporaries to absorb.

Kant also confronts the issue of the power of reason, something much in debate among philosophers of his time. Some find it ironic that a central figure of the Enlightenment,* a movement associated with rational enquiry, actually cast doubt on the cognitive scope of reason (cognition is the mental process of gaining understanding through experience.) In fact, Kant was not the only one. The Scottish radical empiricist* philosopher David Hume* was especially important for Kant. Like other empiricists, Hume found that thought and knowledge originated in perceptual experience: one cannot know, through reason alone, what lies beyond experience. Kant sought to establish definitively what was and was not within the cognitive reach of reason.

Overview of the Field

Kant was steeped in the major philosophical and intellectual currents of the time. In late eighteenth-century Germany, followers of Gottfried Leibniz* and Christian Wolff* dominated the philosophy faculties of German universities. Today scholars regard Leibniz, one of the most influential German philosophers before Kant, as a major figure of the rationalist* school. Leibniz believed that people *could* attain genuine knowledge using reason alone, as in the discipline of mathematics. Indeed, Leibniz viewed mathematics as an important model for all human knowledge.

Leibniz published few philosophical writings. After he died, however, his disciple Wolff produced countless volumes on all manner of topics, philosophical and otherwise. Holding geometrical proofs as the model of rational argumentation, Wolff wrote in a highly systematic* way that imitated those proofs: first he laid down principles and definitions, and then painstakingly derived propositions from them.

Philosophically, the unashamedly metaphysical* Leibnizian-Wolffian school held that reason alone could establish the true nature of the world. Leibniz also held that God coordinates the movements of substances according to a preordained blueprint that he termed "pre-established harmony." In other words, according to Leibniz and Wolff, things do not really interact on their own.

Much of Kant's *Critique* challenges the rationalist school's methodological assumptions and specific metaphysical beliefs. A section of *Critique* entitled "On the Amphiboly of the Concepts of Reflection"[1] directly attacks key theories of Leibniz's philosophy.

Academic Influences

Wolffian rationalism may have been the dominant position in Kant's time, but it was not an unchallenged view. Kant's contemporaries heard and debated a range of ideas that circulated across Europe. One of Kant's main university teachers, philosopher Martin Knutzen* (1713–51), advocated a diverse blend of philosophies. Knutzen's teachings integrated Pietism* (a reform movement that stressed personal religious devotion) and British empiricism (the belief that all ideas derive from sensory experience). These teachings on empiricism focused particularly on the ideas of John Locke.* Knutzen led Kant to doubt such central Leibnizian doctrines as pre-established harmony.

He also kept Kant up to date on modern scientific subjects, especially astronomy and the works of English physicist and mathematician Isaac Newton.* Indeed, Kant made one of his first major intellectual contributions in the field of astronomy. His 1755 essay "Universal History and Theory of the Heavens" anticipated the "nebular hypothesis"*—a theory about the formation and development of the solar system—of French scientist Pierre-Simon de Laplace.*

The theses Kant put forward in *Critique* would certainly have been out of step with those in the standard rationalist textbooks of the time. Yet throughout his career, Kant continued to lecture from such texts, including those of his fellow German Alexander Baumgarten.*

In his *Critique*, Kant questioned many of the rationalists' basic assumptions but his aim was not purely to act as an adversary. *Critique* occupies an intriguing position: agreeing with the rationalists that human reason could achieve more than the British empiricists suspected, and at the same time supporting the empiricists' case that rationalism overstated the pure power of reason. Kant conceived a revolutionary philosophy as an attempt to forge a middle way.

NOTES

1   Immanuel Kant, *Critique of Pure Reason*, trans. Paul Guyer and Allen W. Wood (Cambridge: Cambridge University Press, 1998), A260/B316–A292–B349.

MODULE 3
THE PROBLEM

KEY POINTS

- Major preoccupations of early modern philosophers were the sources of human knowledge.

- While British empiricists* believed that all knowledge derives from experience, rationalists* argued that fundamental components of our knowledge are innate to the mind.

- Kant argued that his predecessors had grasped only half the truth: knowledge requires input from both sensory experience and understanding.

Core Question

In *Critique of Pure Reason*, Immanuel Kant identifies the central question of his project as answering the problem: "How are synthetic *a priori* judgments possible?"[1] *A priori** knowledge can be acquired independently of experience, as opposed to *a posteriori** knowledge, which we acquire through experience. Synthetic judgments* tell us something important about the world because they have a firm basis in reality, and they are not true merely by virtue of meaning. Their opposite, analytic judgments,* are true by virtue of their meaning and what's more, their contradictions are necessarily false.

Analytic judgments merely tell us what we already know: "All bachelors are unmarried." We cannot make new discoveries about unmarried bachelors. Synthetic judgments extend our knowledge. "All roses are red" is not true by definition—and its opposite, "all roses are not red" contains no inherent contradiction.

So when Kant states that he wants to see how synthetic *a priori*

> ❝ In a word, Leibniz intellectualized the appearances, just as Locke sensitivized the concepts of understanding. ❞
>
> Immanuel Kant, *Critique of Pure Reason*

judgments may be possible, he is talking about things that are not true by definition, but which also cannot be contradicted by evidence, since we know them independently of experience.

The question remains central to Kant's argument. He believes that claims of metaphysical* knowledge are themselves synthetic *a priori* judgments. In Kant's view, metaphysics has made no progress since the ancient Greek philosophers first embarked on its study.

Kant describes metaphysics as a "battlefield" of "endless controversies"[2] On one side of the battle, philosophers who assume that people can attain knowledge by using pure reason—Kant labels these thinkers "dogmatists." On the other side are skeptics who question whether we may ever attain knowledge, on the theory that no amount of experience can tell us what is necessarily true of things in general. Further, no experience can tell us, naturally, the truth about transcendent objects of traditional metaphysics. Transcendent objects are things beyond the range of normal or physical human experience, such as God. So how can humans make inferences from facts about objects of experience that transcend experience?

The Participants

Kant presents himself as a constructive mediator between rationalism and empiricism, two philosophical schools whose ideas form the background to the debates of his time. Each of these schools seized upon a single source of human knowledge—reason in the case of rationalism, and sensibility in the case of empiricism—and each insisted that its source sufficed to explain knowledge. While rejecting what he sees as the excesses of these positions, Kant demonstrates that each school has valid ideas—when suitably modified.

Rationalists like German mathematician and philosopher Gottfreid Leibniz* argued that sensations represent nothing but confused and obscure conceptual representations. In Leibniz's view, the ideas of space and motion, for example, come "from the mind itself, for they are ideas of the pure understanding."[3] By contrast, empiricists like the English philosopher John Locke* argued that general representations or concepts are merely abstractions created from sensory material. Locke wrote, "Let us then suppose the mind to be, as we say, white paper void of all characters, without any ideas; how comes it to be furnished? Whence comes it by that vast store, which the busy and boundless fancy of man has painted on it, with an almost endless variety? Whence has it all the materials of reason and knowledge? To this I answer, in one word, from *experience*: in that, all our knowledge is founded; and from that it ultimately derives itself."[4]

At the heart of Kant's mediation is his thesis of the discursivity* of human knowledge. In Kant's view, knowledge needs the cooperation of two separate sources: sensory intuition and conceptual understanding.

The Contemporary Debate

Kant contends that no one before him had ever asked the key question about whether synthetic *a priori* knowledge is possible. If we can understand the nature of synthetic knowledge, he argues, we can ascertain what sorts of things we can have synthetic *a priori* knowledge of. For example, we would be able to validate our synthetic *a priori* judgments about God, or about causality.

Second, Kant argues that previous philosophy has assumed that knowledge is a matter of our judgments conforming to the nature of objects. That is, we acquire knowledge because our judgments correspond to the way things really are. Believing that this assumption lies at the center of philosophy's centuries-old battles, Kant suggests we instead investigate whether objects conform to the very structures of human knowledge.[5] This radical move is the essence of Kant's "Copernican* revolution."

Taking one step back from the objects of metaphysical knowledge themselves, Kant urges philosophers to examine instead the essential intellectual capacities of humans to achieve knowledge of objects. Kant calls this "transcendental" enquiry.* His *Critique* is therefore an investigation not into objects, but into the conditions necessary for human beings to acquire knowledge of objects.

NOTES

1   Immanuel Kant, *Critique of Pure Reason*, trans. Paul Guyer and Allen W. Wood (Cambridge: Cambridge University Press, 1998), B19.

2   Kant, *Critique of Pure Reason*, Aviii.

3   G. W. Leibniz, *New Essays on Human Understanding*, abr. edn, trans. and ed. Peter Remnant and Jonathan Bennett (Cambridge: Cambridge University press, 1981),128.

4   John Locke, *Essay Concerning Human Understanding* (Oxford : Clarendon, 1975), II.I.2.

5   Kant, *Critique of Pure Reason*, Bxvi.

MODULE 4
THE AUTHOR'S CONTRIBUTION

KEY POINTS

- Kant argued that the basic concepts of human understanding constitute objects of experience.

- He introduced a fundamental distinction between appearances and things in themselves.

- Kant explicitly combined key ideas from the philosophies of rationalism* and empiricism* to create his unique philosophy.

Author's Aims

Immanuel Kant's *Critique of Pure Reason*[1] aims to determine the possibility and scope of metaphysics,* that is, of philosophical investigation into the nature of reality.

Most traditional philosophers would begin with an investigation into the objects that supposedly compose reality. Kant does not do this. Instead, he asks what grounds we have to assume that one can ever have true thoughts or "representations" of the traditional objects of metaphysics. These *a priori** constructs do not arise from objects we encounter in experience, nor can they be proven by experiment. Examples of such metaphysical objects include not just the representation of God but also any properties objects possess in general, just by virtue of being objects at all.

So is metaphysics possible? Kant builds his answer around his positive doctrine of transcendental idealism.* This doctrine claims that we can have *a priori* knowledge about appearances, but never about things as they are in themselves.

> **❝** Hence let us once try whether we do not get farther with the problems of metaphysics by assuming that the objects must conform to our cognition, which would agree better with the requested possibility of an *a priori* cognition of them, which is to establish something about objects before they are given to us. **❞**
>
> Immanuel Kant, *Critique of Pure Reason*

Having established his principal aim, Kant details his plan for the work. The central constructive section of *Critique*, the "Transcendental Analytic," covers roughly its first half. In the Analytic, Kant establishes that *a priori* representations belong to two faculties: of sensibility, that is, the capacity to be affected by external objects, and of understanding, that is, of conceptual thought. Kant also outlines which representations—and how many—belong to each faculty. Having established these facts, Kant demonstrates how the representations of the understanding actually refer to the objects they purport to be about.

The less constructive—in fact, more destructive—part of *Critique*, the "Transcendental Dialectic," concerns the *a priori* representations of a third faculty, reason. Reason forms ideas of the objects of special metaphysics, namely God, the soul, and the cosmos. Kant argues that it is impossible to gain *a priori* knowledge of the objects of special metaphysics. However, he recognizes that humans have been tempted by the idea that we can attain metaphysical knowledge. In Kant's view, we cannot ever attain it—and he takes pains to explain why, so we might learn how to avoid the temptation in the future.

Approach

Kant approaches his solution to the problem of synthetic *a priori* judgment by discussing the nature of space and time. In *Inaugural Dissertation*—a work published in 1770, over a decade before

Critique—he argues that both space and time are merely forms through which creatures with our particular subjective constitution represent objects. Humans' sensible representations of objects are therefore limited by these conditions of appearances. At the same time, Kant argues that the concepts we arrive at through pure reason—our rational intellect*—offer us metaphysical knowledge of things as they are in themselves, not just their appearances. By the time he wrote *Critique*, he had abandoned that idea. Kant's later work contends that the intellect's basic concepts yield knowledge only when combined with data given through the senses in what he calls "intuition."

In *Critique*, Kant asks how we can have knowledge not just of how things appear, but of how they are in themselves. If such representations "depend upon our inner activity," he wonders how they can agree with their objects. Usually states of affairs come to agree with our representations through action—when we decide we would like the room to be warmer, we bring the world into alignment with our desires by turning on the heat (or in Kant's day, lighting the fire). If this were the case with metaphysics, we would have to be gods in order to create the objects of experience.

This problem led Kant to the realization that our basic concepts make up objects. We must abandon the idea of knowledge being the mind's attempt to conform to something utterly independent of the mind. Stated most basically, the world as an object of knowledge is not separate from the resources we bring to it. This solution and its complex elaboration are largely original to Kant.

Contribution In Context

Kant's *Critique* belongs primarily to the philosophical sub-disciplines of epistemology* and metaphysics. It has an intriguing relation to epistemology—the study of human knowledge: Kant asks first and foremost not what we can know, but how can we even have thoughts about objects. It doesn't matter whether those thoughts are true or false, only that we have the audacity to believe that we have a right to think them. This reflective or "critical" turn continues to influence philosophers.

Critique has a complex, and largely negative, relation to metaphysics. Traditionally, metaphysicians had debated such topics as whether God exists and whether the universe had a beginning. Here, Kant's originality lay in asking whether these questions were even valid, since their answers lay beyond the bounds of possible human knowledge. Smultaneously though, Kant also showed why we keep asking these unanswerable questions. He argued that humans have a natural interest in them, even though they cannot be answered.

Today, we usually view Kant just as he viewed himself: as someone who synthesized the major philosophical trends of his time, especially rationalism and empiricism, to forge a new position. Rather than belonging to a philosophical school, Kant founded one in his own right. "Kantian" remains an adjective very much in use by both his supporters and his detractors.

NOTES

1 Immanuel Kant, *Critique of Pure Reason*, trans. Paul Guyer and Allen W. Wood (Cambridge: Cambridge University Press, 1998).

SECTION 2
IDEAS

MAIN IDEAS

KEY POINTS

- Kant's key concern in his *Critique* is the actual possibility or otherwise of metaphysics*.

- His doctrine of "transcendental idealism"* states that we can have knowledge only of objects of possible experience, not of things in themselves.

- Kant offers several lines of argument for his core themes, which work together. These include a constructive analysis of our capacity for knowledge as well as critiques of traditional metaphysics.

Key Themes

In his *Critique of Pure Reason,* Immanuel Kant puts forward a theory of human thought and knowledge that he called "transcendental idealism." His theory contains three key ideas.

First, there is Kant's metaphor of a "Copernican revolution"—that his theory changed the discipline of philosophy to the same radical degree that the fifteenth-century astronomer Copernicus upended his contemporaries' traditional ideas about the cosmos. Scholars have interpreted this metaphor in conflicting ways. Fundamentally, Kant was getting at a shift toward a human standpoint or perspective. Copernicus* showed that although it looks as though the Sun moves across the sky every day, in reality, the Earth moves around the Sun— the breakthrough came from a shift in perspective. Similarly, Kant looked to shift the perspective of philosophers. Explaining the nature of the world must come from referencing the human mind.

Second, there is Kant's thesis of the discursivity* of the human

> **❝** Without sensibility no object would be given to us, and without understanding none would be thought. Thoughts without content are empty, intuitions without concepts are blind. **❞**
>
> Immanuel Kant, *Critique of Pure Reason*

intellect. He proposed that human beings possess two sources of knowledge: concepts and intuitions. These roughly correspond to our capacity to think and our capacity to perceive things. In Kant's view, knowledge can arise only when these two capacities function in tandem.

Third, there is Kant's thesis about the nature of the judgments of particular interest to philosophy. The statement "everything has a cause" represents a synthetic* *a priori** judgment—that is, a necessary truth which could not possibly be false. The other kind of judgment Kant outlined is analytic. The statement "bachelors are unmarried" represents an analytic judgment. It is necessarily true: it is impossible to be a married bachelor. Yet unlike "bachelors are unmarried," "everything has a cause" is not simply true by definition. As a synthetic judgment, it tells us something substantive about the world.

Exploring The Ideas

Kant combines these three ideas to explain the possibility of human knowledge, including synthetic *a priori* knowledge. In his view, we are only able to claim knowledge of something when concepts combine with intuitions. Together, concepts and intuitions do not just reflect objects; they actually constitute the objects. In Kant's view, the objects that we see around us would not be the way they are if our concepts were not doing some work. Further, Kant argues that beyond the activity of constituting things, our concepts have no valid application. So we cannot use concepts to gain knowledge that goes beyond experience.

The basic structures of the mind create our objects of experience. Note that just as Copernican astronomy does not question the reality of its object, the Sun, Kant does not claim that objects are simply mental constructs. In his terms, objects are "transcendentally ideal," yet "empirically real." Scholars have struggled to understand exactly what Kant means by this. Kant's contention seems to be that since objects are transcendentally ideal, they are available to us only within a framing conceptual context. If I did not have the right concepts, I would not see ordinary objects like cups and plates as I do. But human beings encounter objects as empirically real in their experience—when I see the cup, it appears to be an object existing outside of me, and not part of my mind.

Freewheeling concepts of understanding alone cannot afford us genuine knowledge unless they are constrained and grounded by perceptual experience. Conversely, we cannot form representations of objects merely through sensation, in which objects somehow impress themselves onto the mind. Our understanding must take an active role in its being affected by objects. Kant writes that "without sensibility no object would be given to us, and without understanding none would be thought."[1]

Kant argues that we are only able to experience objects because we unify information we receive through the senses by applying metaphysical principles. However, beyond this task of unification, metaphysical concepts are, in Kant's words, without "sense and significance."[2]

Language And Expression

The year after Kant published his *Critique*, one reviewer called it a "monument to the nobility and subtlety of the human understanding," but thought it would be "incomprehensible to the greatest majority of the reading public." The reviewer recommended it mainly for "the teachers of metaphysics."[3] This assessment from 1782 stands today.

Students of *Critique* often spend years working through the text; many devote their entire careers to understanding it. The book itself has become identified with complexity and profundity (or what is deep and philosophical).

Kant uses a wide variety of arguments in *Critique*, and he sets them out in notoriously dense sentences. The convoluted language makes any attempt to pin down the text's key ideas extremely difficult. Although it remains a key text for those with serious philosophical interests, *Critique* has not found an audience outside of academia.

The difficulty of reading Kant's *Critique* is made worse by the large number of technical terms he introduces in it. For instance, Kant invented the notion of "transcendental idealism." Difficult as his terminology is, subsequent philosophers have found it useful; they have adopted it as a way of talking about both Kant's ideas and their own.

NOTES

1   Immanuel Kant, *Critique of Pure Reason*, trans. Paul Guyer and Allen W. Wood (Cambridge: Cambridge University Press, 1998), A51/B75.

2   Kant, *Critique of Pure Reason*, B149.

3   Manfred Kuehn, *Kant: A Biography* (Cambridge: Cambridge University Press, 2001), 254.

MODULE 6
SECONDARY IDEAS

KEY POINTS

- Kant argues that our ideas of God, the soul, and the cosmos as a totality arise from a "logic of illusion." Yet he says that it lies in the nature of reason itself to produce these metaphysical* illusions.

- His arguments have led many philosophers to abandon the traditional projects of metaphysics.

- Kant's critique of arguments for the existence of God and the soul contributed to the gradual separation of philosophy and theology* (the study of the nature of God and the doctrines of religion.)

Other Ideas

The "Transcendental Dialectic" section of Immanuel Kant's *Critique of Pure Reason* sets out the author's arguments about metaphysics. Rather than enhancing the store of metaphysical knowledge, as earlier philosophers had attempted to do, Kant offers withering criticisms of the entire discipline.

In this section, the negative connotations of the word "critique" come forward. Kant demonstrates that the knowledge claimed by traditional metaphysics is an illusion. The "Transcendental Dialectic" moved Moses Mendelssohn,* a prominent rationalist* contemporary of Kant, to call him "the all-destroying Kant."[1]

The problem arises because, in Kant's view, we use our concepts in a valid way only when we apply them to intuitions: that is, to experiences. In contrast, traditional metaphysics applies concepts beyond the bounds of all possible human experience. For example,

> ❝ The transcendental dialectic will therefore content itself with uncovering the illusion in transcendental judgments, while at the same time protecting us from being deceived by it; but it can never bring it about that transcendental illusion (like logical illusion) should even disappear and cease to be an illusion. ❞
>
> Immanuel Kant, *Critique of Pure Reason*

metaphysicians speak of a God who transcends the empirical world, or of an original first cause of everything we can experience.

In the "Dialectic," Kant undertakes three tasks. First, he shows that the metaphysical use of concepts leads to various contradictions. Having destroyed the illusion that metaphysics can produce answers, he then attempts to soften the blow by claiming he understands why humans continue to fall for the illusion that metaphysical questions can be answered: we cannot help but try to answer metaphysical questions and the risk of falling into illusion, Kant thinks, "irremediably attaches to human reason."[2] Yet by understanding the intellectual mechanisms responsible for these attempts, we can, in Kant's view, resist the temptation of claiming to have knowledge of the metaphysical. Kant's third and final task in this section is to make the intriguing argument that despite their illusory nature, human beings' ideas of the absolute do play a positive role.

Exploring The Ideas

Kant argues that reason naturally extends the concepts of the understanding to form ideas of "the absolute" or of "unconditioned" objects. For example, reason takes the category, or pure concept, of causality* and seeks an object that does not itself have causal conditions. Such an object would serve as the absolute ground of existing objects subject to causal conditions. Kant sees three ideas of the unconditioned that reason has generated: God, the soul, and the entire cosmos.

First, Kant shows that the metaphysical use of concepts such as causality leads to contradictions. For example, suppose we ask whether or not the universe as a whole had a cause.[3] It cannot have had a cause: if it had, the cause would itself be part of the universe. Still, everything has a cause so the universe must also have one: without a cause, the universe could not have begun.

Second, Kant shows us how to escape the contradictions. Concepts like "cause" properly apply only to objects of possible experience: that is, to things inside the universe. The universe itself, as a whole, is not an object of possible experience. So it does not make sense to ask what the cause of the universe as a whole is.

Finally, Kant shows how the ideas of the unconditioned nevertheless have a use.[4] In the case of causality, the use is as what Kant calls a "regulative idea:" it directs scientific enquiry, since science progresses by understanding more and more about the causal order. Science always asks: what caused this? The ideal of science is that we can understand the causes of everything in the universe. Even if this ideal is never achieved, it spurs our enquiry.

The ideas of the unconditioned also have a moral use. While cognition of the objects of special metaphysics is impossible, we can "think" them according to pure concepts. Kant believes that we must think of unconditioned entities like free will and God in moral contexts.

Overlooked

In recent years, scholars have begun to examine the *Critique* in the light of Kant's earlier, pre-critical works. "Pre-critical" designates the period leading up to the *Inaugural Dissertation* of 1770, before he developed the philosophical ideas he would express in his three critiques, *Critique of Pure Reason* (1781), *Critique of Practical Reason* (1778), and *Critique of Judgment* (1790).

In part, this scholarship has challenged a prevailing idea about Kant's development. According to this story, Kant was a complacent rationalist metaphysician. He was stripped of his uncritical naivety after reading the works of rationalist David Hume.* Rethinking his past completely, he wrote the philosophy for which he would become famous. However, other recent studies of Kant's philosophical development emphasize the relative continuity of his thought over the decades. In this view, the critical works result from a gradual evolution rather than a radical rupture.[5]

Another effect of these studies has been to reassess the importance of Leibniz's* influence on Kant. Some scholars now see rationalist metaphysics not only as the target of the critique, but also as an integral part of its constructive doctrine. Such readings often challenge rival contemporary interpretations that emphasize Kant's anti-metaphysical credentials.[6]

NOTES

1 Lewis White Beck, *Early German Philosophy* (Cambridge, MA: Belknap Press of Harvard University Press, 1969), 337.

2 Immanuel Kant, *Critique of Pure Reason*, trans. Paul Guyer and Allen W. Wood (Cambridge: Cambridge University Press, 1998), A298/B354.

3 For Kant's discussion of causality, see the "Third Antinomy" in the *Critique of Pure Reason*, A444/B472.

4 Kant, *Critique of Pure Reason*, A642/B670ff.

5 See Alison Laywine, *Kant's Early Metaphysics and the Origins of the Critical Philosophy*, North American Kant Society Studies 3 (Atascadero, CA: Ridgeview, 2003), and Martin Schönfeld, *The Philosophy of the Young Kant: The Precritical Project* (Oxford: Oxford University Press, 2000).

6 See, for example, Rae Langton, *Kantian Humility: Our Ignorance of Things in Themselves* (Oxford: Clarendon Press, 1998).

ACHIEVEMENT

KEY POINTS

- Following the publication of the *Critique*, generations of philosophers became skeptical about the possibility of traditional metaphysics.*

- Kant's key idea that concepts must relate to experience in order to have "sense and reference" has had enduring power.

- The strict division Kant made between appearances and unknowable things in themselves has been a constant obstacle to the acceptance of his own brand of idealism.

Assessing The Argument

One modern-day Immanuel Kant scholar, British philosopher Sebastian Gardner, aptly described the impact of *Critique of Pure Reason*: "It would be hard to exaggerate the importance of Kant's philosophy; hardly any major philosophical movement since the end of the eighteenth century can claim to have shielded itself from his influence. Kant rewrote the history of modern philosophy in a way that made it impossible to conscientiously revert to earlier modes of philosophising."[1] Kant's influence on nineteenth-century German philosophers like Georg Hegel* is obvious, because they explicitly expanded on his work, but his influence can also be seen in much less obvious places, for example in the twentieth-century work of American philosopher Wilfrid Sellars* and Austrian-British philosopher Ludwig Wittgenstein.*

After Kant's *Critique*, philosophers simply never returned to doing metaphysics in the traditional fashion. Even those who still wish to

> ❝ In spite of some sympathy shown in recent years for a vaguely Kantian sort of idealism or, better, anti-realism, which argues for the dependence of our conception of reality in our concepts and/or linguistic practices, Kant's transcendental idealism proper, with its distinction between appearances and things in themselves, remains highly unpopular. ❞
>
> Henry E. Allison, *Kant's Transcendental Idealism: An Interpretation and Defense*

pursue metaphysical enquiry take Kant's arguments seriously.

That is not to say that every philosopher influenced by Kant accepts his views wholesale. Kant himself made that difficult to do. One obstacle is the distinction Kant made between appearances and things as they are in themselves. According to one interpretation, Kant says both that appearances comprise a kind of replica world, and that we cannot be certain of the existence of the world of which it is a replica. Scholars have seen this as an unbelievable doctrine.

In the twentieth century, philosophers such as Gerold Prauss[*2] in Germany and Graham Bird[*3] in the UK have steadily contested this reading. This school has developed an alternative revisionist interpretation that reads Kant as rejecting any replication of worlds. A recent scholar working in this area of interpretation is the US philosopher Henry Allison.[4] In his interpretation of Kant, there is only one world, but the world has two aspects. That is, we can consider the world in two distinct ways: as it appears to us and as it would be if we were not around to experience it.

Achievement In Context

Over time, scholars have changed their evaluations of the significance of *Critique*'s contribution to philosophy. Such changes are unsurprising.

Kant wrote a subtle text, treating a variety of topics in a very loosely systematic way. In doing this, he challenges the reader to identify what lies at *Critique*'s philosophical center and what is on the edge.

Even *Critique*'s famous destruction of rationalist* theology* is ambiguous. Many have read it as striking a blow to religion. But in the nineteenth century, German philosopher Friedrich Nietzsche* saw Kant's philosophy as offering a gift to German Protestantism.* Just when the forces of Enlightenment* threatened traditional religious doctrines, Kant rescued God and the immortal soul by placing them beyond the boundaries of strict knowledge while preserving them as objects of moral thought. In Nietzsche's view, Kant insulated theology from its philosophical opponents.

The young German idealists* Friedrich Schelling* and Georg Hegel* approached Kant from a different perspective to Nietzsche. But while studying at the Protestant seminary at Tübingen, they shared his view. Their traditionalist teachers argued that Kant's philosophy offered an opportunity to justify theological dogma—principles laid down by an authority, in this case the Church—as absolutely true.

The way German idealists looked at Kant shows us another way scholars have changed their understanding and views of the *Critique*. Beginning with Austrian philosopher K. L. Reinhold,* who died just two decades after Kant, idealists criticized the work for not being more rigorously systematic. In their view, the work failed to offer a complete list of metaphysical categories or to make clear how they are deduced. In general, they thought Kant's entire philosophy lacked a single unifying principle from which to derive its secondary principles.

More recent Kantians, however, tend to see *Critique*'s very loosely systematic nature as a philosophical virtue. Rather than standing or falling as a tightly integrated whole, in their view, *Critique* allows readers to apply its transcendental methodology independently to different aspects of cognition. In other words, it's not an all-or-nothing proposition. You may disagree with aspects of Kant's philosophy but still derive some benefits from it.

Limitations

Many modern philosophers have questioned Kant's claims to universality. The twentieth-century Scottish moral philosopher Alasdair MacIntyre,* for example, raises two crucial objections. First, he argues that the historicist* tradition of attaching great importance to history, beginning most prominently with Hegel,* has made apparent that "what Kant presented as the universal and necessary principle of the human mind turned out in fact to be principles specific to particular times, places and stages of human activity and enquiry." Thus, "what Kant took to be the principles and presuppositions of natural science as such turned out after all to be the principles and presuppositions specific to Newtonian physics."[5]

Second, MacIntyre finds Kant's separation of necessary principles—the *a priori** and the universal on the one hand and a body of changeable empirical beliefs on the other—to be unsustainable. For evidence of this, he points to the fact that Kant's followers have not stayed true to his philosophy in its original form. Instead, they have produced successively less radical formulations of Kantian doctrines, such as those developed by neo-Kantianism* in the late nineteenth and early twentieth centuries. To MacIntyre, this proves that Kant did not develop universal principles. While we cannot work out the rational validity of universal principles once and for all, their universality consists in how they overcome problems thrown up by previous principles.

Scholars have criticized Kant's conception of reason in culturally specific ways. For example, postcolonial* critiques—the discussion of colonial legacies or the results of one country acquiring control of another country— see Kant's Enlightenment* conceptions as expressions of Western notions of reason whose pretensions to universality are rooted in political motivations. The Enlightenment claimed to be a universal movement, relating to all peoples of the world. But its thinkers sometimes suppressed alternative theories by insisting they were irrational. Interestingly, however, some recent scholarship by philosopher and Kant biographer Martin Schönfeld,* among others, demonstrates Kant's subconscious debt to other philosophies. Noting that traces of Eastern (for example, Chinese) thought appear in Kant's work, these scholars argue that Kant should be seen in a Eurasian, not simply Western, context.[6]

NOTES

1   Sebastian Gardner, *Kant and the Critique of Pure Reason* (London: Routledge, 1999), 327.

2   See Gerold Prauss, *Erscheinung bei Kant : Ein Problem der Kritik der reinen Vernunft* (Berlin: De Gruyter, 1971), and Gerold Prauss, *Kant und das Problem der Dinge an sich* (Bonn: Bouvier, 1977).

3   See Graham Bird, *Kant's Theory of Knowledge: An Outline of One Central Argument in the "Critique of Pure Reason"* (London: Routledge & Kegan Paul, 1962).

4   See Henry E. Allison, *Kant's Transcendental Idealism: An Interpretation and Defence* (New Haven, CT: Yale University Press, 2004).

5   Alasdair MacIntyre, *After Virtue: A Study in Moral Theory,* 2nd edn (London: Duckworth, 1984), 266.

6   Martin Schönfeld (ed.), "Kant and Confucianism," Special Issue, *Journal of Chinese Philosophy* 33, no. 1 (2006): 1–157.

MODULE 8
PLACE IN THE AUTHOR'S WORK

KEY POINTS

- Kant's critical philosophy is devoted to determining the scope and validity of the fundamental principles of the rational mind.
- *Critique of Pure Reason* set the conceptual framework for Kant's entire mature philosophical work.
- Together with his main writings in moral philosophy, *Critique* remains Kant's most enduringly influential work.

Positioning

Immanuel Kant's *Critique of Pure Reason* is the work of a mature thinker. Published in 1781, when Kant was 57, it brought to a close the "silent decade" during which he published relatively little. It is the first of his "critical works," those writings that brought him to philosophical prominence and for which he is still best known: *Critique of Pure Reason*, *Critique of Practical Reason*, and *Critique of Judgment*. By the early 1790s, Kant himself thought his intellectual powers were beginning to wane, although he continued to write significant pieces.

Critique of Pure Reason provides the basic philosophical framework for Kant's later critical works. In particular, it establishes the epistemological* restrictions within which they must operate. These restrictions center on the subtle view that while we can have genuine knowledge only of appearances, we can nonetheless think about things in themselves.[1] This doctrine is vital to Kant's work in other areas, from ethics, to philosophy of religion, to aesthetics*—the philosophical study of either beauty or art.

Interestingly, *Critique of Pure Reason* seems to exclude the possibility

> ** All interest of my reason (the speculative as well as the practical) is united in the following three questions:
>
> 1. What can I know?
>
> 2. What should I do?
>
> 3. What may I hope? **
>
> Immanuel Kant, *Critique of Pure Reason*

of a critique of aesthetic judgment. In a famous footnote, Kant states that no philosophical *a priori** principles govern judgments of beauty.[2] Less than a decade later, he had obviously changed his mind, as he set forth aesthetic principles in his 1790 *Critique of Judgment*.

Integration

Critique of Pure Reason began a new phase in Kant's intellectual life. While he lays out its arguments in a loosely systematic manner, his subsequent works are, for the most part, tightly organized. In many ways, the later works develop the arguments of *Critique of Pure Reason*.

His second critical work, *Critique of Practical Reason*, published in 1788, contains Kant's moral theory. He introduced many of its themes in the first *Critique*. For example, in *Pure Reason*'s section on the "third antinomy," Kant addresses the opposition of freedom and determinism.* Determinism for Kant is the theory that every event has a cause, and the connection between cause and effect falls under a natural law. Proving that transcendental freedom[3] of the will is metaphysically impossible, he discusses its moral implications. In the "Doctrine of Method" at the end of the book, Kant discusses the nature of moral laws, moral motivation, and the traditional concept of the "highest good." Many of the later work's central ideas respond to puzzles brought up in the first *Critique*.

In 1787, Kant brought out a second edition of *Critique of Pure*

Reason. The most important of his revisions involves the section on transcendental deduction,[4] often considered to be the work's philosophical centerpiece. Feeling that many readers had failed to understand the new form of idealism* he proposed, Kant rewrote the section completely. Scholars still debate the philosophical differences between the two editions. Some claim that the rewritten material simply offers the same argument, but with a different mode of presentation.[5]

A more recent scholarly debate about the development of Kant's thought concerns his late unpublished manuscripts, known as the *Opus Postumum.* In these writings, some scholars claim, Kant frequently reconsiders some key critical doctrines.[6]

Significance

It is hard to overstate the impact that Kant's critical works have had on European philosophy. The subsequent history of philosophy can often be talked about in terms of reactions to and reworkings of his ideas. For example, the materialist* reaction to post-Kantian idealism in nineteenth-century Germany (materialism being the view that reality consists exclusively of physical matter) was followed by the "back to Kant" mindset of Neo-Kantians* like German philosophers Ernst Cassirer* and Paul Natorp,* who wielded a great deal of influence in late nineteenth- and early twentieth-century philosophy. This dynamic pattern has recurred in new forms, and philosophers continue to generate variants of Kantianism up to the present day.

Critique of Pure Reason remains Kant's most significant single work. The only other works of his that could compare are those on moral theory. The most important of these may be *Groundwork for the Metaphysics of Morals* (1785) and *Critique of Practical Reason* (1788). These works develop Kant's views on practical, as opposed to theoretical, reason. Practical reasoning is the reasoning we engage in when deciding how to act. Theoretical reasoning, by contrast, is crucial to science: it is the reasoning we engage in when deciding what is true. Kant believed that his critical philosophy held the key to both forms of reasoning.

NOTES

1   Immanuel Kant, *Critique of Pure Reason*, trans. Paul Guyer and Allen W. Wood (Cambridge: Cambridge University Press, 1998), Bxxvi.

2   Kant, *Critique of Pure Reason*, A21/B35.

3   For Kant, true freedom requires transcendental freedom, that is, the ability of the will to determine actions independently of the influence of the mechanical causes which govern nature.

4   The "Transcendental Deduction" is the usual abbreviation for the chapter of the *Critique of Pure Reason* entitled "Transcendental Deduction of the Pure Concepts of the Understanding." In this chapter, Kant seeks to prove that the categories, or basic concepts, of the faculty of the understanding are valid for experience. Kant completely rewrote the deduction for the second edition of the work.

5   See Graham Bird, *The Revolutionary Kant: A Commentary on the Critique of Pure Reason* (Chicago: Open Court, 2006).

6   See Eckart Förster, *Kant's Final Synthesis: An Essay on the Opus Postumum* (Cambridge, MA: Harvard University Press, 2000).

SECTION 3
IMPACT

THE FIRST RESPONSES

KEY POINTS

- Many of Kant's first readers thought he offered just another version of philosopher George Berkeley's* idealism,* a denial that objects exist outside of our representations.

- To combat early misinterpretations, Kant wrote the *Prolegomena to any Future Metaphysics* as an introduction to his philosophy. He also significantly revised *Critique* for a second edition.

- The subtle and ambiguous nature of Kant's idealism presents a puzzle to his readers, both in his day and in ours.

Criticism

One of the first reviews of Immanuel Kant's *Critique of Pure Reason* was published anonymously in January 1782 in the *Göttingische Gelehrte Anzeigen*. Its author was later revealed to be the German philosopher Christian Garve.* Garve's review associated *Critique* with the writings of British empiricism,* especially those of Anglo-Irish cleric and philosopher George Berkeley and Scottish philosopher David Hume.*

Berkeley's idealism held that to be is to be perceived, and so the world is made up of our ideas. Hume advanced a skeptical thesis that many of our beliefs about the world stem neither from experience nor reason. They arise from the way our minds work. In short, we hold the beliefs we do because of human nature.

Garve, and the other early reviewers who followed his lead ,misunderstood a crucial point. *Critique of Pure Reason* does *not* offer a

> ❝ When the *Critique* first appeared, Kant expected not only that he would be understood, but also that other scholars would rally to support his project. ❞
>
> Manfred Kuehn, *Kant: A Biography*

metaphysical account of what objects are. It instead investigates our *a priori** concepts of objects in general.

In time, more sympathetic readers began to respond to Kant's book. The efforts of eighteenth-century Austrian philosopher Karl Leonhard Reinhold* were especially important in this regard. In such works as *Letters on the Kantian Philosophy*, Reinhold did much to popularize Kant's doctrines—in the process, becoming an intellectual celebrity in his own right. Although Reinhold did not present *Critique* in all its sophistication, and in fact subjected it to several amendments, his reception of Kantianism would be a crucial impetus in the development of German idealism.

Responses

The reviews greatly disappointed Kant. He had expected scholars to welcome his book. He believed they would applaud the innovative means by which he proposed to end age-old disputes in metaphysics.* He thought his fellow philosophers would rush to spread his new doctrines. Sadly, he was mistaken.

Kant was also confused when he discovered that Christian Garve had written the anonymous *Göttingen* review. Kant had expected that Garve, like his fellow German philosopher Moses Mendelssohn,* would both understand and promote *Critique*. Mendelssohn, Kant learned, was too ill to pay much attention to his work, and it emerged that Garve's criticism had been significantly revised and shortened by the journal's editor, Johan Feder.*

The Garve–Feder review, as it is now known, had important

consequences for Kant. Regarding his theoretical philosophy, Garve questioned whether Kant had the resources to distinguish between objective experience and mere fantasy or dreams. Addressing this criticism led Kant to the theory of physical bodies he would provide in the 1786 *Metaphysical Foundations of Natural Science*. Garve also found Kant's account of moral motivation and of the relation between theology* and ethics inadequate. Kant would not solve these issues to his own satisfaction until he came to write *Critique of Practical Reason* in 1787.

Conflict And Consensus

Dismayed that the initial reception of his *Critique* associated his philosophy with that of the British empiricist philosophers Berkeley and Hume, Kant published the *Prolegomena to any Future Metaphysics* in 1783. Written in clearer, more accessible language than the *Critique*, Kant used the *Prolegomena* to stress his differences from Hume. Kant did this by placing the question of the possibility of synthetic* *a priori** judgments at the center of the work. Some have argued that Hume— who died five years before Kant published *Critique*—would not have been skeptical about the possibility of metaphysical judgments if he had understood their synthetic *a priori* nature. If Hume had followed that line of reasoning, he would have hit upon the doctrine of *Critique*: that the necessity of such judgments lies in the faculty of understanding itself.

When he prepared *Critique*'s second edition in 1787, Kant added a "Refutation of Idealism" designed to distance himself from what he calls Descartes's* problematic idealism and Berkeley's dogmatic idealism.[1] As articulated by sixteenth-century philosopher René Descartes, problematic idealism denies that we can infer the existence of a real external world from our perceptions and beliefs. For the problematic idealist, we do not know whether the external world exists. Dogmatic idealism reduces outer objects to modifications of inner sense and thereby asserts that being is identical to being perceived.

In revising his work for the second edition, Kant generally sought to downplay the idealist elements of his position.[2] For example, besides adding the "Refutation," he famously rewrote the transcendental deduction of the categories. These demonstrate the objective validity of the understanding's pure concepts. The differences between the two versions of the deduction remain topics of scholarly debate. But the second edition deduction reads much less like a psychological account of the mechanisms involved in cognition than its first-edition counterpart. This change further distanced Kant's transcendental project from what he regarded as Hume's psychological mode of explanation.

NOTES

1   Immanuel Kant, *Critique of Pure Reason*, trans. Paul Guyer and Allen W. Wood (Cambridge: Cambridge University Press, 1998), B274–279.

2   Manfred Kuehn, *Kant: A Biography* (Cambridge: Cambridge University Press, 2001), 311

MODULE 10
THE EVOLVING DEBATE

KEY POINTS

- Kant's idea, that our knowledge of reality is a joint function of the external world and of the resources we bring to it, has provided the basic example for much subsequent philosophy.

- Both German idealism* in the early nineteenth century and Neo-Kantianism* in the late nineteenth and early twentieth centuries emerged from Kant's critical philosophy.

- *Critique* has had a vast impact on subsequent philosophers, influencing movements from phenomenology* to communicative rationality theory* and philosophers as diverse as Gottlob Frege* and Martin Heidegger.*

Uses And Problems

Scholars commonly understand the history of nineteenth-century philosophy in terms of its Kantian heritage. The course of German philosophy during that century is especially significant in this regard. Supporters of the post-Kantian movement known as German idealism, which dominated German philosophy in the early nineteenth century, saw themselves as completing Kant's project. After the 1830s, however, anti-idealism arose, beginning with the work of Ludwig Feuerbach.* Varieties of naturalism* and materialism* attempted to use the ever-progressing natural sciences to account for human knowledge.

Later, Neo-Kantianism arose to challenge naturalism. Scholars like Paul Natorp* and Ernst Cassirer* initiated a so-called "back to Kant"

> ❝ The effect of Kant was indeed exceptional. One cannot be pleased that, fifty years after the appearance of Kant, after we are admittedly at a different point, but one to which we would never have got *without* him, Kant's contribution is diminished by those who contribute nothing to going beyond Kant. ❞
>
> F. W. J. Schelling, *On the History of Modern Philosophy*

movement. Attacking the naivety of the naturalists, they re-established a Kantian dividing line between science and philosophy. Unlike the naturalists, they followed Kant in stressing the limits of empirical knowledge. They demonstrated how scientific theorizing and investigation take place within conceptual frameworks contributed by human understanding. They also followed Kant in arguing that human cognition could not be reduced to material processes.

Late nineteenth-century philosophers such as Franz Brentano* restored Kant's distinction between subjective processes involved in thinking, which can be empirically investigated, and the conditions of thoughts having objective content, which cannot. The logical innovations of Gottlob Frege, often considered the founder of analytic philosophy,* and of Edmund Husserl,* who founded the phenomenological school of philosophy, both depend upon this basic distinction.

Of course, scholars in other countries also studied and reacted to Kant. But it is important to understand the history of philosophy in Germany because German idealism, especially the work of Hegel,* exercised an immense influence on twentieth-century philosophy across Europe. Husserl's philosophy of phenomenology counted several major European thinkers among its devotees, from Germany's Martin Heidegger to France's Jean-Paul Sartre.* Tracing the way *Critique* has been received reveals significant movements in the history of philosophy of the past two centuries.

Schools Of Thought

Fewer explicitly Kantian schools of thought appeared in the twentieth century. Instead, *Critique*'s influence showed itself in subtler ways. Various philosophers updated its arguments with the help of modern philosophical tools and logic.

Within English-speaking circles, *Critique* had to overcome certain philosophical tendencies that ran counter to its own. Bertrand Russell,* for example, a founding father of analytic* philosophy, explicitly wished to return modern philosophy to its eighteenth-century roots.[1] The roots Russell had in mind stretched back to the pre-Kantian eighteenth century, particularly the empiricism* of Scottish philosopher David Hume.*

In contrast to Kant's systematic ambitions, English-speaking philosophy favored a piecemeal approach. Supporters of the new analytic school rejected the so-called idealist philosophies of the late nineteenth century. Reaching further back in history, they also frequently dismissed Kant's doctrine of transcendental idealism.* Analytic philosophy was generally hostile to metaphysics* and analytic philosophers considered Kant's division of things in themselves and appearances a grand metaphysical thesis. Analytic philosophy favored the philosophical tool of conceptual analysis. This appeared incompatible with Kant's method of transcendental investigation into the rational mind. Not until the second half of the twentieth century did analytic philosophers return in larger numbers to the philosophy of *Critique*.

In the second half of the twentieth century, philosophers became more receptive to Kant's thoughts. British philosopher and metaphysician Jonathan Bennett's* *Kant's Analytic*[2] and his countryman Peter Strawson's* *The Bounds of Sense*[3] prompted the reevaluation. Strawson claimed that his work discarded Kant's elaborate transcendental apparatus. Instead, Strawson focused on the core argument of *Critique*. Analyzing the necessary components and suppositions of our concept of experience, Strawson claimed to offer, in a Kantian spirit, a descriptive rather than a revisionary metaphysics. A descriptive metaphysics analyzes the fundamental conceptual scheme we require for consciousness of objects, rather than making recommendations about how we should revise our notions of the way things really are. Strawson's approach spawned a considerable literature on "transcendental arguments"—arguments that start with features of experience to deduce ways the world must be if we are to count those experiences as accurate. A wide range of scholars became concerned about the nature of these arguments and their power to refute skepticism.

In Current Scholarship

The American philosopher Wilfrid Sellars* has also revived interest in *Critique*. His highly original use of Kant in texts such as *Science and Metaphysics: Variations on Kantian Themes*[4] updated *Critique* with the tools of pragmatist* philosophy and modern logic and philosophy of language. Sellars is himself an innovator in these fields.

Sellars used his embrace of Kant's Copernican* revolution to attack a variety of empiricist assumptions. Noting that humans bring to our experience a sophisticated, holistic web of rules, Sellars sought to demonstrate how those rules make various central cognitive dimensions of human experience available to us. I can only see perceptual experience as providing evidence for beliefs, for example, if I already use my knowledge of the world to interpret my perceptual experience. The work of many influential philosophers around the world, such as the American Jay Rosenberg and the South African John McDowell,* have built on Sellars's innovations

Kant's *Critique* has exercised a vast influence on philosophy in continental Europe. The prominent contemporary German philosopher Jürgen Habermas* has developed a theory of rationality along broadly Kantian lines. Habermas stresses the themes of inter-subjective* validity and rational convergence. He also notes the transcendental conditions of asserting validity claims across a range of debates—including not only the empirical sciences, but also our thought about morality and art. In specifying such conditions, however, Habermas strays from Kant and from his strong claims to universal and necessary principles. Also unlike Kant, Habermas does not consider philosophy foundational and autonomous, or as acting on its own. Habermas therefore focuses on empirical and hypothetical knowledge. He embraces a more pragmatic methodology, drawing on a range of resources from the social sciences to linguistics.

NOTES

1 See Kenneth Westphal, "Kant's *Critique of Pure Reason* and Analytic Philosophy," in *The Cambridge Companion to Kant's Critique of Pure Reason*, ed. Paul Guyer (Cambridge: Cambridge University Press, 2010), 401–31.

2 Jonathan Bennett, *Kant's Analytic* (Cambridge: Cambridge University Press, 1966).

3 Peter Strawson, *The Bounds of Sense: An Essay on Kant's "Critique of Pure Reason"* (London: Methuen, 1975).

4 Wilfrid Sellars, *Science and Metaphysics: Variations on Kantian Themes* (London: Routledge & Kegan Paul; New York: Humanities Press, 1968).

IMPACT AND INFLUENCE TODAY

KEY POINTS

- *Critique* continues to influence work across philosophical disciplines, from epistemology* to the philosophy of language.
- Its arguments remain a challenge to contemporary work in metaphysics* and the theory of knowledge.
- The widespread attempt to understand the mind purely in natural scientific terms presents a considerable challenge to contemporary Kantianism.

Position

Philosophical preoccupations and fashions always change. But scholars continue to find ways to apply Immanuel Kant's *Critique of Pure Reason* in new areas, from philosophy of science, to the problem of intentionality,* to cognitive science.*

The revival in Kant scholarship over the past few decades has given philosophers greater access to both its arguments and Kant's intentions, enabling Kant to inspire further philosophical developments. In particular, an approach pioneered by twentieth-century scholars such as Gerold Prauss[1] and Graham Bird[2] has offered a "deflationary" reading of Kant's transcendental idealism* that some consider metaphysically plausible.

Through much of the last century, scholars dismissed Kant's notorious division of appearances and things in themselves—and, by extension Kantian idealism. The concept seemed an implausible mixture of metaphysics and crippling skepticism. The deflationary

> **"**Aside from some Kant scholars, there are not many philosophers who still believe that Kant proved in this argument that we possess synthetic *a priori* knowledge, although there is wide admiration for the power of Kant's arguments about, at least, causality and substance. But there remains a great deal of interest in his basic picture of the nature of conscious mindedness. **"**
>
> Robert Pippin, *Hegel on Self-Consciousness*

approach, however, presents transcendental idealism as a metaphysically neutral doctrine that sees appearances and things in themselves as two aspects of, or two ways of considering, objects. Such sophisticated accounts of his philosophy have encouraged contemporary scholars to reexamine Kant.

Philosophers today mine *Critique* for potential solutions to contemporary problems. The prominent contemporary philosopher John McDowell,* for example, has written, "Kant should still have a central place in our discussion of the way thought bears on reality."[3] Relevant topics for this discussion include Kant's theory of intentionality, that is, of how conscious states can be about or directed towards objects. Contemporary philosophers are also reexamining Kant's theory of self-consciousness and its relation to the consciousness of objects. Kant's theory of concept-formation and his account of how concepts are necessarily related to judgments also have relevance.

Modern philosophers continue to debate how concepts possess content through playing a role within a structured thought by uniting or, in Kant's language, "synthesizing" many concepts.

Interaction

Contemporary thinkers and schools have adopted many of *Critique*'s ideas. For example, philosophers who want to preserve a notion of the mind's rational autonomy often prize its theory of the mind. They embrace Kant's argument that self-conscious judgment about the world requires subjects to actively apply standardizing rules. The rules we apply in making empirical judgments must not, Kant argues, be rules derived from further rules. Higher-order rules specify necessities that structure our experience of an objective world. In Kant's view, they cannot be merely psychological; they must be rational and conceptual. Higher-order rules escape investigations that dig beyond the level of rational conceptual activity, attempting to explain knowledge in merely causal terms.

Those thinkers who adopt this set of commitments follow the intentions of Kant's text. In part, their work restages Kant's battle against the unrestricted empiricism* of his own day. The emerging sciences of the seventeenth and eighteenth centuries understood the world as a series of mechanisms. British empiricists of the time, such as John Locke* and David Hume,* sought to apply this mechanistic view to the human mind. With *Critique*, Kant intended to combat such mechanistic and merely causal accounts of rationality.

Critique informs our contemporary intellectual environment by, among other things, resisting attempts to explain rational activity solely in terms of the natural sciences. Practitioners in the fields of neuroscience,* evolutionary psychology* and other disciplines continue this pursuit. Kant has stood against this approach for more than three centuries.

The Continuing Debate

The central ideas of Kant's *Critique of Pure Reason* are important in a variety of contemporary discussions. American philosopher Hilary Putnam* offers one example of how Kantian ideas function in modern debates.

The "internal realism"* Putnam developed in the 1980s made an explicit appeal to Kant's critical philosophy. Kant had put forward the idea that since the inputs we receive from a causally independent world are not independent of our conceptual schemes, they do not require any single, exclusive system of concepts. Putnam argued in favor of this position. In his view, Kantian ideas can help combat the contention that these conceptual systems or schemes are ultimately contingent and relative—or that underlying sub-rational factors such as sociological, ideological, or psychological forces determine them.

Ideological and political concerns often motivate the people responding to the Kantian position today. People often attack Kant's high Enlightenment* faith in reason, either implicitly or explicitly. In particular, they mention Kant's claim to have articulated necessary and universal principles. Modern philosophers sometimes view this as an attempt to exert undue influence and quash alternative ideas.

Postmodernist* theorists, for example, have challenged Kant's fundamental assumption that reason can investigate and ground itself. While they regard other mental capacities mentioned by Kant as fundamental—such as the imagination and the power of judgment—they place reason in a lower position.[4] Connected with this challenge is an assault on the Kantian conception of the thinking subject. Postmodernists have tried to displace the self-sufficient, autonomous Kantian reason. Instead, they theorize the self as an unstable and essentially variable product of factors extending beyond it, whether social, political, economic, or psychological.

As is so often the case, given his considerable historical influence, even Kant's critics have been influenced by his thought. Postmodernism radicalizes Kant's idea that we do not know things as they are in themselves, but only in terms of the subjective positions to which they are given. Those taking this position maintain that any distinction between the natural and the artificial is itself artificial. Anything utterly non-artificial would be illusory in itself. Against this background, postmodernists suggest that basic metaphysical concepts, including the self, are less necessary and considerably more fluid than we—and Kant—suspected.

NOTES

1   See Gerold Prauss, *Erscheinung bei Kant : Ein Problem der Kritik der reinen Vernunft* (Berlin: De Gruyter, 1971), and Gerold Prauss, *Kant und das Problem der Dinge an sich* (Bonn: Bouvier, 1977).

2   See Graham Bird, *Kant's Theory of Knowledge: An Outline of One Central Argument in the "Critique of Pure Reason"* (London: Routledge & Kegan Paul, 1962).

3   John McDowell, *Mind and World* (Cambridge, MA: Harvard University Press, 1994), 3.

4   See, for example, Jean-François Lyotard, *The Postmodern Condition: A Report on Knowledge*, trans. Geoff Bennington and Brian Massumi (Minneapolis: University of Minnesota Press, 1984).

WHERE NEXT?

KEY POINTS

- *Critique* is likely to have an enduring influence across philosophical traditions.

- The text remains relevant beyond its importance as an historical reference point. Philosophers continue to interpret and defend many of its central arguments.

- In *Critique,* Kant raises fundamentally new questions about the nature of human knowledge and reconceives the relationship between mind and world.

Potential

The ideas of Immanuel Kant's *Critique of Pure Reason* have gone in and out of fashion throughout the past two centuries. In the early twentieth century, for example, German philosopher Gottlob Frege's* work on the development of logic appeared to go against Kant's derivation of the categories—the pure concepts of the understanding. Kant had adapted these fundamental forms of judgment using the traditional logic of Greek philosopher Aristotle.* Yet recent scholarship has defended Kant's way of doing things in the light of modern logic.[1]

Another common twentieth-century view has been that the development of non-Euclidean geometry* and Einstein's theory of relativity* rendered Kant's theories of space and time redundant. Yet recent commentators have argued that, if suitably modified, central aspects of Kant's views on the spatial and temporal nature of our intuition are indeed compatible with modern scientific knowledge.

In *Critique,* Kant mediated between different philosophical schools and theories. The sophistication of these arguments has also

> ❝There are limits to what we can conceive of, or make intelligible to ourselves, as a possible general structure of experience. The investigation of these limits, the investigation of the set of ideas which forms the limiting framework of all our thought about the world and experience of the world, is, evidently, an important and interesting philosophical undertaking. No philosopher has made a more strenuous attempt on it than Kant. ❞
>
> Peter Strawson, *The Bounds of Sense*

contributed to *Critique*'s staying power: its theories allow for differing emphases. So when the philosophical world was hostile to metaphysics,* Kantians emphasized Kant's own criticisms of traditional metaphysics. They presented his transcendental idealism* as a strictly neutral view.[2] On the other hand, philosophers more amenable to the practice of metaphysics have read Kant's transcendental idealism as being more metaphysically pronounced.

Another sign of *Critique*'s continuing adaptability are contemporary readings that approach the text using tools from disciplines that simply did not exist in Kant's day. Critics once dismissed Kant's investigation of a human's cognitive* capacities as a fanciful "transcendental psychology." Some scholars today have looked at *Critique* and have highlighted modern naturalistic approaches to the theory of knowledge. They draw, for example, on work from cognitive science and artificial intelligence.*[3] New approaches to human cognition may well continue to find unexpected connections to Kant.

Future Directions

Many of the text's disciples are philosophers developing novel positions in their own right. Often such scholars come to *Critique* already possessing knowledge of how generations of former disciples have interpreted it. The University of Pittsburgh philosophers John McDowell* and Robert Brandom* are two of many like this.

Both Brandom and McDowell examine the nature of human thought, understanding, and reason. Though their philosophies are significantly different, both find these things absolutely governed by rules and structured by concepts. In recent years, McDowell has developed an account of perception that takes forward Kant's theory of the relation between passive receptivity and spontaneous mental activity in perceptual experience.[4] Brandom, who sees himself as working in the pragmatist* tradition, has developed an "inferentialist" semantics* that allows us to determine the meaning of expressions by how they are used to infer things within a language. He has drawn significantly upon Kant's work.[5]

Both philosophers represent a broader trend among *Critique*'s current disciples. Instead of viewing the text as an attempt to confront Cartesian* skeptical questions—such as how we might move out from an inner mental realm to an objective, external world—they stress that Kant's primary philosophical aim in *Critique* is to offer a theory of intentionality.* Kant, it is now commonly claimed, focused philosophy on the question of how our minds can bear upon objects at all. He wondered how we can entertain thoughts about the world in the first place, whether those thoughts are true or false.

Kant's *Critique*, therefore, continues to find new and ingenious disciples, not only amongst those who are studying his work, but also among today's leading philosophers. These people bring their own innovative resources to the text. They have brought Kantian thinking to the modern day as they explore philosophy of content, of perception, of normativity and also to the fundamental question of how human reason fits into and relates to nature.

Summary

Immanuel Kant led an uneventful life. The first modern philosopher to have a conventional university post as almost his exclusive profession, he seldom strayed from his hometown of Königsberg. Yet his best works have had an unparalleled impact on subsequent philosophy. *Critique of Pure Reason* stands at the heart of these works.

With *Critique*, Kant claimed to have effected a revolution in philosophy similar to that of Copernicus* when he placed the Sun rather than Earth at the center of the universe. Whether subsequent thinkers have accepted or rejected Kant's reorientation of philosophy, it is difficult to argue against the fact that he has been behind a constant philosophical line of thinking during the past two centuries. Kant's name and ideas continue to pop up in all manner of philosophical writings.

Kant's idea that the world is as much a function of the resources we bring to it as of what it brings to us is ingrained in our intellectual culture. This concept has not only altered philosophy, it has also informed a host of subsequently emerging disciplines for which it, mostly without knowing it, provided the essential intellectual backdrop.

Yes, in some respects previous thinkers anticipated Kant's intellectual revolution. None however, came close to articulating their ideas with the imaginative originality or argumentative power that Kant musters in *Critique of Pure Reason*.

NOTES

1   See Michael Wolff, *Die Vollständigkeit der Kantischen Urteilstafel: mit einem Essay über Freges Begriffsschrift* (Frankfurt am Main: Klostermann, 1995).

2   The principal text of this movement is Henry E. Allison, *Kant's Transcendental Idealism: An Interpretation and Defence* (New Haven, CT: Yale University Press, 2004).

3   See, for example, Patricia Kitcher, *Kant's Transcendental Psychology* (New York: Oxford University Press, 1990).

4   John McDowell, *Having the World in View: Essays on Kant, Hegel and Sellars* (Cambridge, MA: Harvard University Press, 2009).

5   See Robert Brandom, *Reason in Philosophy: Animating Ideas* (Cambridge, MA: Belknap Press of Harvard University Press, 2009).

GLOSSARY

GLOSSARY OF TERMS

Aesthetics: the philosophical study of either beauty or art.

Analytic judgments: judgments that are true by virtue of the meaning of their terms. For example, "all bachelors are unmarried" is true because "bachelor" means, in part, "unmarried."

Analytic philosophy: originally, the program of solving philosophical problems by the logical analysis of language. Figures such as Bertrand Russell (1872–1970), Rudolf Carnap (1891–1970) and Ludwig Wittgenstein (1889–1951) founded this school of thought. Subsequent English-language philosophy is often referred to as "analytic," yet scholars dispute whether or not this implies anything more than a geographical designation.

A posteriori **knowledge:** knowledge acquired from sensory experience.

A priori **knowledge:** knowledge that can be acquired independently of sensory experience.

Artificial Intelligence: the notion and development of computers that are able to perform tasks that are considered to require human intelligence. This could be decision-making and translating between languages.

Cartesianism: the philosophical and mathematical ideas of René Descartes (1596–1650). As Descartes is commonly dubbed the "father of modern philosophy," much subsequent Western philosophy, especially of the seventeenth and eighteenth centuries, tends to be understood against the background of his ideas. In particular, scholars debate his contention that mind and body are really distinct substances.

Cognitive science: the interdisciplinary study of the mind, encompassing parts of psychology, philosophy, linguistics, and computer science.

Communicative rationality theory: the theory that understands human rationality as a necessary outcome of successful communication.

Determinism: for Kant, the theory that every event has a cause, and the connection between cause and effect falls under a natural law.

Discursivity: knowledge is discursive, in Kant's view, because it requires both intuitions (perceptual experiences of the world) and concepts (general categories which we apply to things).

East Prussia: part of the historical region of Prussia situated along the south-eastern Baltic coast. The province of East Prussia became part of the German state of Prussia, with its capital in Königsberg, after the first partition of Poland in 1772. After World War II, Joseph Stalin divided the territory between Poland and the Soviet Union.

Empiricism: a position in the theory of knowledge, holding that all knowledge derives from sensory experience.

Enlightenment: a cultural and intellectual movement in seventeenth- and eighteenth-century Europe and North America. The movement was devoted to the combat of irrationality, superstition, and arbitrary political authority.

Epistemology: the philosophical study of the nature of knowledge and of the justification of belief.

Evolutionary psychology: the psychological study of how humans adapt mentally to a changing environment.

German idealism: an intellectual movement that arose in the wake of Kant's critical philosophy. Its central members were Johann Gottlieb Fichte (1762–1814), Friedrich Wilhelm Joseph Schelling (1775–1854) and George Wilhelm Friedrich Hegel (1770–1831).

Historicism: a general name for philosophical views that attach great importance to history.

Idealism: an extremely flexible term within philosophy. While it generally denotes some form of dependence upon mind or reason, its meaning varies according to context and from philosopher to philosopher. Kant's transcendental idealism is formal, and scholars continue to debate the precise meaning of this formal idealism. But it appears that Kant believes the structures of human reason and intuition provides the form of objects (but not their material).

Inferentialist semantics: the view that the meaning of an expression should be understood in terms of its inferential roles with other expressions, rather than its truth conditions.

Intentionality: the object-directedness or "aboutness" of a state. Fear is intentional, for example, insofar as it is fear *of* something.

Internal realism: The concept, initially put forward by neo-Kantian Hilary Putnam, that conceptual systems are independent—not contingent and relative, and not determined by underlying sub-rational factors such as sociological, ideological, or psychological forces.

Inter-subjective: something (often a concept) that is comprehensible to a number of people.

Materialism: the view that reality consists exclusively of physical matter.

Metaphysics: the philosophical study of the ultimate nature of reality or being. In Kant's day, it embraced "general metaphysics," or ontology, and "special metaphysics." "General metaphysics" specifies the categories of being and so the nature of objects in general. "Special metaphysics" concerns the nature of specific entities: the world, the soul, and God.

Naturalism: an extremely broad term in modern philosophy that has no single meaning. Very broadly speaking, forms of substantive naturalism, which allow only those entities sanctioned by the natural sciences into scientific explanations. Methodological naturalism attempts to solve philosophical problems using only methods sanctioned by the natural sciences.

Nebular hypothesis: a theory about the formation and development of the solar system. Kant argued that rotating gaseous clouds—nebulae—form stars and planets. Nebulae collapse under the force of gravity.

Neo-Kantianism: a movement beginning in the 1860s and lasting until the early twentieth century that returned to Kantian doctrines in reaction to the materialism of mid-nineteenth-century German philosophy. Its main centers were in Marburg and Baden in the south-west of Germany. Prominent Neo-Kantians included Hermann Cohen (1842–1918) and Heinrich Rickert (1863–1936).

Neuroscience: a field of study incorporating the scientific disciplines concerned with the nervous system.

Non-Euclidian geometry: geometry that differs from the notions of Euclid, especially that only one line may be drawn through a given point parallel to a given line.

Phenomenology: the study of consciousness and the objects of direct experience.

***Philosophes*:** prominent French representatives of the ideals of the Enlightenment. Scholars still debate the question of who merits inclusion as a *philosophe*. But the group's famous members are commonly said to include the playwright, philosopher, and historian François-Marie Arouet, known as Voltaire (1694–1778); philosopher, art critic, and writer Denis Diderot (1713–84); and philosopher, mathematician, and physicist Jean Le Rond d'Alembert (1717–83).

Pietism: the Pietists were a Lutheran reform movement that stressed personal piety, religious experience, and the role of conscience in the religious life.

Postcolonial studies: the analysis of the cultural, social, and political legacy of colonialism and imperialism.

Postmodernism: a diffuse variety of schools of thought within philosophy, cultural and political theory, and the humanities that came to prominence in the 1980s. The term is notoriously difficult to define. It is just as notoriously difficult to isolate thinkers who accept the label. Two who are less controversially associated with postmodernism are the Italian philosopher and politician Gianni Vattimo (born 1936) and French philosopher and literary theorist Jean-François Lyotard (1924–98).

Pragmatism: a philosophical position that originated in the United States in the late nineteenth century. It seeks to elucidate concepts of philosophical concern, especially knowledge and truth, in terms of their practical consequences and efficacy.

Protestantism: a variety of forms of Christianity emerging from or subsequent to the Protestant Reformation. The German monk Martin Luther (1483–1546) criticized several doctrines and practices of the medieval Catholic Church. After he was condemned as a heretic, his followers started protests that eventually led to the end of the Catholic Church's monopoly on Christianity.

Rationalism: an early-modern philosophical school. The rationalists gave their philosophical proofs a rigorous, quasi-mathematical structure. Unlike empiricists, they believed that some knowledge was innate to human reason. The most important rationalists were René Descartes (1596–1650), Baruch Spinoza (1632–77), and Gottfried Wilhelm von Leibniz (1646–1716).

Substance: the nature of substance was a common and controversial theme in early modern philosophy. Generally speaking it is that in which the properties of an object inhere, or become fixed.

Synthetic judgments: judgments which, unlike analytic judgments, are not true by virtue of the meaning of their terms, but rather give substantive information about the world.

Systematicity: the quality or condition of being systematic.

Theology: the discipline devoted to explaining the nature of God or the divine as well as the doctrines of religions quite generally.

Theory of relativity: two theories of the mathematician and physicist Albert Einstein, the theory of special relativity published in 1905 and the theory of general relativity published in 1916.

Transcendental enquiry: enquiry not into the world itself, but into the conditions under which we can acquire knowledge of the world.

PEOPLE MENTIONED IN THE TEXT

Aristotle (384–322 b.c.e.) was a Greek philosopher and scientist who is still to this day one of the most respected thinkers in these fields.

Alexander Gottlieb Baumgarten (1716–62) was a German philosopher. He is principally remembered as the author of the *Aesthetica* (1750–8) that is generally regarded as a foundational work of modern Western aesthetics.

Jonathan Bennett (b. 1930) is a British philosopher of language and metaphysics who has written about Kant. He has a website dedicated to making philosophy texts more accessible.

George Berkeley (1685–1753) was an Irish empiricist philosopher and bishop. He is known for the theory of "immaterialism" which he expounded in his *A Treatise Concerning the Principles of Human Knowledge* (1710).

Robert Brandom (b. 1950) is an American philosopher. He is best known for his book *Making it Explicit* (1994).

Franz Brentano (1838–1917) was a German philosopher and psychologist. His works include *Psychology from an Empirical Standpoint* (1874) and *The Classification of Mental Phenomena* (1911).

Ernst Cassirer (1874–1945) was a Polish philosopher who wrote *Kant's Life and Thought,* and later expanded on Kant's ideas by focusing on symbols and the philosophy of mathematics.

Nicolaus Copernicus (1473–1543) was a Polish astronomer and mathematician. His 1543 work *De Revolutionibus Orbium Coelestium* (*On the Revolutions of the Celestial Spheres*) propounded the thesis that the Earth revolves around the Sun. Copernicus's work is considered to be foundational for modern science.

René Descartes (1596–1650) was a French philosopher and mathematician. Often referred to as the father of modern philosophy, he is best known for his *Discourse on Method* (1637) and *Meditations* (1641).

Gottlob Frege (1848–1925) was a German philosopher, logician, and mathematician. His innovations in logic and the philosophy of language were foundational for modern analytic philosophy. His works include *The Foundations of Arithmetic* (1884) and several important articles such as "On Sense and Reference" (1892).

Christian Garve (1742–98) was a German Enlightenment philosopher and translator. Heavily influenced by contemporary British philosophy, Garve was one of Kant's most significant critics.

Jürgen Habermas (b. 1929) is a German philosopher and sociologist working within the tradition of critical theory. His works include *The Theory of Communicative Action* (1981) and *The Philosophical Discourse of Modernity* (1985).

George Wilhelm Friedrich Hegel (1770–1831) was a German idealist philosopher. His works include *The Phenomenology of Spirit* (1807) and *The Science of Logic* (1812–17).

Martin Heidegger (1889–1976) was a German philosopher. His best-known work is *Being and Time* (1927). Amongst his later works are studies of other philosophers, including *Kant and the Problem of Metaphysics* (1929).

David Hume (1711–76) was a Scottish empiricist philosopher and historian. His philosophy is most extensively elaborated in his *A Treatise of Human Nature* (1739).

Edmund Husserl (1859–1938) was a German philosopher and mathematician. Known as the founder of phenomenology, his works include *Logical Investigations* (1900–1) and *Cartesian Meditations* (1931).

Martin Knutzen (1713–51) was a German philosopher who taught at the University of Königsberg. A disciple of Alexander Baumgarten, he is principally known today as a teacher of Kant.

Pierre-Simon, Marquis de Laplace (1749–1827) was a French mathematician and astronomer. He is known for his many innovations in mathematics and natural science and for his five-volume *Celestial Mechanics* (1798–1827).

Gottfried Wilhem von Leibniz (1646–1716) was a German philosopher and a key figure in the rationalist movement of early modern philosophy. A hugely prolific author, he is known for his *Monadology* (1714) and *Theodicy* (1709).

John Locke (1632–1704) was an English empiricist philosopher and political theorist. He is best known for his *An Essay Concerning Human Understanding* (1689) and *Two Treatises of Government* (1689).

Alasdair MacIntyre (b. 1929) is a Scottish philosopher best known for *After Virtue* (1985).

John McDowell (b. 1942) is a British philosopher. His works include *Mind and World* (1994).

Moses Mendelssohn (1729–86) was a German philosopher. The major figure of the so-called *haskalah*, the Jewish Enlightenment of the eighteenth century, he is the author of *Jerusalem* (1783) and *Phäedon or On the Immortality of Souls* (1767).

Paul Natorp (1854–1924) was a German philosopher who co-founded the Marburg school of philosophy that revived Kant's theories.

Isaac Newton (1642–1727) was an English mathematician and physicist. His *Philosophiae Naturalis Principia Mathematica* (1687) laid the foundations for classical mechanics. Both he and Gottfried Wilhelm Leibniz independently discovered the infinitesimal calculus.

Friedrich Nietzsche (1844–1900) was a German philosopher and philologist. His principal works include *Thus Spoke Zarathustra* (1883–5) and *Beyond Good and Evil* (1886).

Hilary Putnam (b. 1926) is an American philosopher. His works include *Reason, Truth and History* (1981) and *The Threefold Cord: Mind, Body, and World* (1999).

Karl Leonhard Reinhold (1757–1823) was an Austrian philosopher and early champion of Kantianism. His attempt to unify Kant's philosophy with a single principle in his *Essay Towards a New Theory of the Faculty of Representation* (1789) was a key influence on German idealism.

Bertrand Russell (1872–1970) was a British philosopher. His works include the three-volume *Principia Mathematica* (1910–13) (co-authored with Alfred North Whitehead) and *The Analysis of Mind* (1921).

Jean–Paul Sartre (1905–80) was France's most prominent post-World War II public intellectual. He wrote plays, novels, screenplays, and journalism as well as philosophical treatises. A prominent exponent of existentialist philosophy and Marxism, his best-known philosophical works are *Being and Nothingness* (1943), *Existentialism is a Humanism* (1946), and *The Critique of Dialectical Reason* (1960). *Being and Nothingness* falls into the phenomenological tradition of Edmund Husserl and Martin Heidegger, yet is replete with Hegelian themes.

Friedrich Wilhelm Joseph Schelling (1775–1854) was a German idealist philosopher. His works include the *System of Transcendental Idealism* (1800) and *The Ages of the World* (1811–15).

Martin Schönfeld teaches in the department of philosophy at the University of South Florida. He wrote his PhD thesis on Kant and has also published his own work on him, *The Philosophy of the Young Kant* (2000).

Wilfrid Sellars (1912–89) was an American pragmatist philosopher. His works include *Empiricism and the Philosophy of Mind* (1956).

Peter Strawson (1919–2006) was a British philosopher who worked at Oxford University and was knighted for services to philosophy in 1977.

Christian Wolff (1679–1754) was a German philosopher. He was a disciple of Leibniz and expositor of his works. Little read today, he was a major force in eighteenth-century German philosophy and author of a vast number of works on most of the scholarly subjects of his day.

WORKS CITED

WORKS CITED

Allison, Henry E. *Kant's Transcendental Idealism: An Interpretation and Defense*. New Haven, CT: Yale University Press, 2004.

Beiser, Frederick C. *The Fate of Reason: German Philosophy from Kant to Fichte*. Cambridge, MA: Harvard University Press, 1987.

Bennett, Jonathan. *Kant's Analytic*. Cambridge: Cambridge University Press, 1966.

Bird, Graham. *Kant's Theory of Knowledge: An Outline of One Central Argument in the "Critique of Pure Reason."* London: Routledge & Kegan Paul, 1962.

The Revolutionary Kant: A Commentary on the Critique of Pure Reason. Chicago: Open Court, 2006.

Brandom, Robert. *Reason in Philosophy: Animating Ideas*. Cambridge, MA: Belknap Press of Harvard University Press, 2009.

Cavell, Stanley. *Must We Mean What We Say: A Book of Essays*. Cambridge: Cambridge University Press, 1976.

Förster, Eckart. *Kant's Final Synthesis: An Essay on the Opus Postumum*. Cambridge, MA: Harvard University Press, 2000.

Forster, Michael N. *Kant and Skepticism*. Princeton, NJ: Princeton University Press, 2008.

Kant, Immanuel. *Critique of Pure Reason*. Translated by Paul Guyer and Allen W. Wood. Cambridge: Cambridge University Press, 1998.

Correspondence. Translated and edited by Arnulf Zweig. Cambridge: Cambridge University Press, 1999.

Theoretical Philosophy after 1781. Edited by Henry Allison and Peter Heath. Translated by Gary Hatfield et al. Cambridge: Cambridge University Press, 2002.

Kuehn, Manfred. *Kant: A Biography*. Cambridge: Cambridge University Press, 2001.

Langton, Rae. *Kantian Humility: Our Ignorance of Things in Themselves*. Oxford: Clarendon Press, 1998.

Laywine, Alison. *Kant's Early Metaphysics and the Origins of the Critical Philosophy*. North American Kant Society Studies in Philosophy 3, Atascadero, CA: Ridgeview, 1993.

Lukes, Steven. Émile Durkheim: His Life and Work: A Historical and Critical Study. Harmondsworth: Penguin Books, 1975.

Lyotard, Jean-François. *The Postmodern Condition: A Report on Knowledge.* Translated by Geoff Bennington and Brian Massumi. Minneapolis: University of Minnesota Press, 1984.

MacIntyre, Alasdair. *After Virtue: A Study in Moral Theory.* London: Gerald *Duckworth* & Co., 1985.

McDowell, John. *Mind and World.* Cambridge, MA: Harvard University Press, 1994.

Having the World in View: Essays on Kant, Hegel and Sellars. Cambridge, MA: Harvard University Press, 2009.

Prauss, Gerold. *Erscheinung bei Kant : Ein Problem der Kritik der reinen Vernunft.* Berlin: De Gruyter, 1971.

Kant und das Problem der Dinge an sich. Bonn: Bouvier Verlag, 1977.

Putnam, Hilary. *Reason, Truth and History.* Cambridge: Cambridge University Press, 1981.

Schönfeld, Martin *The Philosophy of the Young Kant: The Precritical Project.* Oxford: Oxford University Press, 2000

ed., "Kant and Confucianism," Special Issue, *Journal of Chinese Philosophy* 33, no 1 (2006): 1–157.

Sellars, Wilfrid. *Science and Metaphysics: Variations on Kantian Themes.* London: Routledge & Kegan Paul, and New York: Humanities Press, 1968.

Strawson, Peter. *The Bounds of Sense: An Essay on Kant's "Critique of Pure Reason."* London: Methuen, 1975.

Westphal, Kenneth. "Kant's *Critique of Pure Reason and Analytic Philosophy.*" In *The Cambridge Companion to Kant's Critique of Pure Reason*, edited by Paul Guyer, 401–31. Cambridge: Cambridge University Press, 2010.

Wolff, Michael. *Die Vollständigkeit der kantischen Urteilstafel: mit einem Essay über Freges Begriffsschrift.* Frankfurt am Main: Klostermann, 1995.

THE MACAT LIBRARY
BY DISCIPLINE

AFRICANA STUDIES

Chinua Achebe's *An Image of Africa: Racism in Conrad's Heart of Darkness*
W. E. B. Du Bois's *The Souls of Black Folk*
Zora Neale Huston's *Characteristics of Negro Expression*
Martin Luther King Jr's *Why We Can't Wait*
Toni Morrison's *Playing in the Dark: Whiteness in the American Literary Imagination*

ANTHROPOLOGY

Arjun Appadurai's *Modernity at Large: Cultural Dimensions of Globalisation*
Philippe Ariès's *Centuries of Childhood*
Franz Boas's *Race, Language and Culture*
Kim Chan & Renée Mauborgne's *Blue Ocean Strategy*
Jared Diamond's *Guns, Germs & Steel: the Fate of Human Societies*
Jared Diamond's *Collapse: How Societies Choose to Fail or Survive*
E. E. Evans-Pritchard's *Witchcraft, Oracles and Magic Among the Azande*
James Ferguson's *The Anti-Politics Machine*
Clifford Geertz's *The Interpretation of Cultures*
David Graeber's *Debt: the First 5000 Years*
Karen Ho's *Liquidated: An Ethnography of Wall Street*
Geert Hofstede's *Culture's Consequences: Comparing Values, Behaviors, Institutes and Organizations across Nations*
Claude Lévi-Strauss's *Structural Anthropology*
Jay Macleod's *Ain't No Makin' It: Aspirations and Attainment in a Low-Income Neighborhood*
Saba Mahmood's *The Politics of Piety: The Islamic Revival and the Feminist Subject*
Marcel Mauss's *The Gift*

BUSINESS

Jean Lave & Etienne Wenger's *Situated Learning*
Theodore Levitt's *Marketing Myopia*
Burton G. Malkiel's *A Random Walk Down Wall Street*
Douglas McGregor's *The Human Side of Enterprise*
Michael Porter's *Competitive Strategy: Creating and Sustaining Superior Performance*
John Kotter's *Leading Change*
C. K. Prahalad & Gary Hamel's *The Core Competence of the Corporation*

CRIMINOLOGY

Michelle Alexander's *The New Jim Crow: Mass Incarceration in the Age of Colorblindness*
Michael R. Gottfredson & Travis Hirschi's *A General Theory of Crime*
Richard Herrnstein & Charles A. Murray's *The Bell Curve: Intelligence and Class Structure in American Life*
Elizabeth Loftus's *Eyewitness Testimony*
Jay Macleod's *Ain't No Makin' It: Aspirations and Attainment in a Low-Income Neighborhood*
Philip Zimbardo's *The Lucifer Effect*

ECONOMICS

Janet Abu-Lughod's *Before European Hegemony*
Ha-Joon Chang's *Kicking Away the Ladder*
David Brion Davis's *The Problem of Slavery in the Age of Revolution*
Milton Friedman's *The Role of Monetary Policy*
Milton Friedman's *Capitalism and Freedom*
David Graeber's *Debt: the First 5000 Years*
Friedrich Hayek's *The Road to Serfdom*
Karen Ho's *Liquidated: An Ethnography of Wall Street*

John Maynard Keynes's *The General Theory of Employment, Interest and Money*
Charles P. Kindleberger's *Manias, Panics and Crashes*
Robert Lucas's *Why Doesn't Capital Flow from Rich to Poor Countries?*
Burton G. Malkiel's *A Random Walk Down Wall Street*
Thomas Robert Malthus's *An Essay on the Principle of Population*
Karl Marx's *Capital*
Thomas Piketty's *Capital in the Twenty-First Century*
Amartya Sen's *Development as Freedom*
Adam Smith's *The Wealth of Nations*
Nassim Nicholas Taleb's *The Black Swan: The Impact of the Highly Improbable*
Amos Tversky's & Daniel Kahneman's *Judgment under Uncertainty: Heuristics and Biases*
Mahbub Ul Haq's *Reflections on Human Development*
Max Weber's *The Protestant Ethic and the Spirit of Capitalism*

FEMINISM AND GENDER STUDIES

Judith Butler's *Gender Trouble*
Simone De Beauvoir's *The Second Sex*
Michel Foucault's *History of Sexuality*
Betty Friedan's *The Feminine Mystique*
Saba Mahmood's *The Politics of Piety: The Islamic Revival and the Feminist Subject*
Joan Wallach Scott's *Gender and the Politics of History*
Mary Wollstonecraft's *A Vindication of the Rights of Woman*
Virginia Woolf's *A Room of One's Own*

GEOGRAPHY

The Brundtland Report's *Our Common Future*
Rachel Carson's *Silent Spring*
Charles Darwin's *On the Origin of Species*
James Ferguson's *The Anti-Politics Machine*
Jane Jacobs's *The Death and Life of Great American Cities*
James Lovelock's *Gaia: A New Look at Life on Earth*
Amartya Sen's *Development as Freedom*
Mathis Wackernagel & William Rees's *Our Ecological Footprint*

HISTORY

Janet Abu-Lughod's *Before European Hegemony*
Benedict Anderson's *Imagined Communities*
Bernard Bailyn's *The Ideological Origins of the American Revolution*
Hanna Batatu's *The Old Social Classes And The Revolutionary Movements Of Iraq*
Christopher Browning's *Ordinary Men: Reserve Police Batallion 101 and the Final Solution in Poland*
Edmund Burke's *Reflections on the Revolution in France*
William Cronon's *Nature's Metropolis: Chicago And The Great West*
Alfred W. Crosby's *The Columbian Exchange*
Hamid Dabashi's *Iran: A People Interrupted*
David Brion Davis's *The Problem of Slavery in the Age of Revolution*
Nathalie Zemon Davis's *The Return of Martin Guerre*
Jared Diamond's *Guns, Germs & Steel: the Fate of Human Societies*
Frank Dikotter's *Mao's Great Famine*
John W Dower's *War Without Mercy: Race And Power In The Pacific War*
W. E. B. Du Bois's *The Souls of Black Folk*
Richard J. Evans's *In Defence of History*
Lucien Febvre's *The Problem of Unbelief in the 16th Century*
Sheila Fitzpatrick's *Everyday Stalinism*

The Macat Library By Discipline

Eric Foner's *Reconstruction: America's Unfinished Revolution, 1863-1877*
Michel Foucault's *Discipline and Punish*
Michel Foucault's *History of Sexuality*
Francis Fukuyama's *The End of History and the Last Man*
John Lewis Gaddis's *We Now Know: Rethinking Cold War History*
Ernest Gellner's *Nations and Nationalism*
Eugene Genovese's *Roll, Jordan, Roll: The World the Slaves Made*
Carlo Ginzburg's *The Night Battles*
Daniel Goldhagen's *Hitler's Willing Executioners*
Jack Goldstone's *Revolution and Rebellion in the Early Modern World*
Antonio Gramsci's *The Prison Notebooks*
Alexander Hamilton, John Jay & James Madison's *The Federalist Papers*
Christopher Hill's *The World Turned Upside Down*
Carole Hillenbrand's *The Crusades: Islamic Perspectives*
Thomas Hobbes's *Leviathan*
Eric Hobsbawm's *The Age Of Revolution*
John A. Hobson's *Imperialism: A Study*
Albert Hourani's *History of the Arab Peoples*
Samuel P. Huntington's *The Clash of Civilizations and the Remaking of World Order*
C. L. R. James's *The Black Jacobins*
Tony Judt's *Postwar: A History of Europe Since 1945*
Ernst Kantorowicz's *The King's Two Bodies: A Study in Medieval Political Theology*
Paul Kennedy's *The Rise and Fall of the Great Powers*
Ian Kershaw's *The "Hitler Myth": Image and Reality in the Third Reich*
John Maynard Keynes's *The General Theory of Employment, Interest and Money*
Charles P. Kindleberger's *Manias, Panics and Crashes*
Martin Luther King Jr's *Why We Can't Wait*
Henry Kissinger's *World Order: Reflections on the Character of Nations and the Course of History*
Thomas Kuhn's *The Structure of Scientific Revolutions*
Georges Lefebvre's *The Coming of the French Revolution*
John Locke's *Two Treatises of Government*
Niccolò Machiavelli's *The Prince*
Thomas Robert Malthus's *An Essay on the Principle of Population*
Mahmood Mamdani's *Citizen and Subject: Contemporary Africa And The Legacy Of Late Colonialism*
Karl Marx's *Capital*
Stanley Milgram's *Obedience to Authority*
John Stuart Mill's *On Liberty*
Thomas Paine's *Common Sense*
Thomas Paine's *Rights of Man*
Geoffrey Parker's *Global Crisis: War, Climate Change and Catastrophe in the Seventeenth Century*
Jonathan Riley-Smith's *The First Crusade and the Idea of Crusading*
Jean-Jacques Rousseau's *The Social Contract*
Joan Wallach Scott's *Gender and the Politics of History*
Theda Skocpol's *States and Social Revolutions*
Adam Smith's *The Wealth of Nations*
Timothy Snyder's *Bloodlands: Europe Between Hitler and Stalin*
Sun Tzu's *The Art of War*
Keith Thomas's *Religion and the Decline of Magic*
Thucydides's *The History of the Peloponnesian War*
Frederick Jackson Turner's *The Significance of the Frontier in American History*
Odd Arne Westad's *The Global Cold War: Third World Interventions And The Making Of Our Times*

LITERATURE

Chinua Achebe's *An Image of Africa: Racism in Conrad's Heart of Darkness*
Roland Barthes's *Mythologies*
Homi K. Bhabha's *The Location of Culture*
Judith Butler's *Gender Trouble*
Simone De Beauvoir's *The Second Sex*
Ferdinand De Saussure's *Course in General Linguistics*
T. S. Eliot's *The Sacred Wood: Essays on Poetry and Criticism*
Zora Neale Huston's *Characteristics of Negro Expression*
Toni Morrison's *Playing in the Dark: Whiteness in the American Literary Imagination*
Edward Said's *Orientalism*
Gayatri Chakravorty Spivak's *Can the Subaltern Speak?*
Mary Wollstonecraft's *A Vindication of the Rights of Women*
Virginia Woolf's *A Room of One's Own*

PHILOSOPHY

Elizabeth Anscombe's *Modern Moral Philosophy*
Hannah Arendt's *The Human Condition*
Aristotle's *Metaphysics*
Aristotle's *Nicomachean Ethics*
Edmund Gettier's *Is Justified True Belief Knowledge?*
Georg Wilhelm Friedrich Hegel's *Phenomenology of Spirit*
David Hume's *Dialogues Concerning Natural Religion*
David Hume's *The Enquiry for Human Understanding*
Immanuel Kant's *Religion within the Boundaries of Mere Reason*
Immanuel Kant's *Critique of Pure Reason*
Søren Kierkegaard's *The Sickness Unto Death*
Søren Kierkegaard's *Fear and Trembling*
C. S. Lewis's *The Abolition of Man*
Alasdair MacIntyre's *After Virtue*
Marcus Aurelius's *Meditations*
Friedrich Nietzsche's *On the Genealogy of Morality*
Friedrich Nietzsche's *Beyond Good and Evil*
Plato's *Republic*
Plato's *Symposium*
Jean-Jacques Rousseau's *The Social Contract*
Gilbert Ryle's *The Concept of Mind*
Baruch Spinoza's *Ethics*
Sun Tzu's *The Art of War*
Ludwig Wittgenstein's *Philosophical Investigations*

POLITICS

Benedict Anderson's *Imagined Communities*
Aristotle's *Politics*
Bernard Bailyn's *The Ideological Origins of the American Revolution*
Edmund Burke's *Reflections on the Revolution in France*
John C. Calhoun's *A Disquisition on Government*
Ha-Joon Chang's *Kicking Away the Ladder*
Hamid Dabashi's *Iran: A People Interrupted*
Hamid Dabashi's *Theology of Discontent: The Ideological Foundation of the Islamic Revolution in Iran*
Robert Dahl's *Democracy and its Critics*
Robert Dahl's *Who Governs?*
David Brion Davis's *The Problem of Slavery in the Age of Revolution*

The Macat Library By Discipline

Alexis De Tocqueville's *Democracy in America*
James Ferguson's *The Anti-Politics Machine*
Frank Dikotter's *Mao's Great Famine*
Sheila Fitzpatrick's *Everyday Stalinism*
Eric Foner's *Reconstruction: America's Unfinished Revolution, 1863-1877*
Milton Friedman's *Capitalism and Freedom*
Francis Fukuyama's *The End of History and the Last Man*
John Lewis Gaddis's *We Now Know: Rethinking Cold War History*
Ernest Gellner's *Nations and Nationalism*
David Graeber's *Debt: the First 5000 Years*
Antonio Gramsci's *The Prison Notebooks*
Alexander Hamilton, John Jay & James Madison's *The Federalist Papers*
Friedrich Hayek's *The Road to Serfdom*
Christopher Hill's *The World Turned Upside Down*
Thomas Hobbes's *Leviathan*
John A. Hobson's *Imperialism: A Study*
Samuel P. Huntington's *The Clash of Civilizations and the Remaking of World Order*
Tony Judt's *Postwar: A History of Europe Since 1945*
David C. Kang's *China Rising: Peace, Power and Order in East Asia*
Paul Kennedy's *The Rise and Fall of Great Powers*
Robert Keohane's *After Hegemony*
Martin Luther King Jr.'s *Why We Can't Wait*
Henry Kissinger's *World Order: Reflections on the Character of Nations and the Course of History*
John Locke's *Two Treatises of Government*
Niccolò Machiavelli's *The Prince*
Thomas Robert Malthus's *An Essay on the Principle of Population*
Mahmood Mamdani's *Citizen and Subject: Contemporary Africa And The Legacy Of Late Colonialism*
Karl Marx's *Capital*
John Stuart Mill's *On Liberty*
John Stuart Mill's *Utilitarianism*
Hans Morgenthau's *Politics Among Nations*
Thomas Paine's *Common Sense*
Thomas Paine's *Rights of Man*
Thomas Piketty's *Capital in the Twenty-First Century*
Robert D. Putman's *Bowling Alone*
John Rawls's *Theory of Justice*
Jean-Jacques Rousseau's *The Social Contract*
Theda Skocpol's *States and Social Revolutions*
Adam Smith's *The Wealth of Nations*
Sun Tzu's *The Art of War*
Henry David Thoreau's *Civil Disobedience*
Thucydides's *The History of the Peloponnesian War*
Kenneth Waltz's *Theory of International Politics*
Max Weber's *Politics as a Vocation*
Odd Arne Westad's *The Global Cold War: Third World Interventions And The Making Of Our Times*

POSTCOLONIAL STUDIES

Roland Barthes's *Mythologies*
Frantz Fanon's *Black Skin, White Masks*
Homi K. Bhabha's *The Location of Culture*
Gustavo Gutiérrez's *A Theology of Liberation*
Edward Said's *Orientalism*
Gayatri Chakravorty Spivak's *Can the Subaltern Speak?*

PSYCHOLOGY

Gordon Allport's *The Nature of Prejudice*
Alan Baddeley & Graham Hitch's *Aggression: A Social Learning Analysis*
Albert Bandura's *Aggression: A Social Learning Analysis*
Leon Festinger's *A Theory of Cognitive Dissonance*
Sigmund Freud's *The Interpretation of Dreams*
Betty Friedan's *The Feminine Mystique*
Michael R. Gottfredson & Travis Hirschi's *A General Theory of Crime*
Eric Hoffer's *The True Believer: Thoughts on the Nature of Mass Movements*
William James's *Principles of Psychology*
Elizabeth Loftus's *Eyewitness Testimony*
A. H. Maslow's *A Theory of Human Motivation*
Stanley Milgram's *Obedience to Authority*
Steven Pinker's *The Better Angels of Our Nature*
Oliver Sacks's *The Man Who Mistook His Wife For a Hat*
Richard Thaler & Cass Sunstein's *Nudge: Improving Decisions About Health, Wealth and Happiness*
Amos Tversky's *Judgment under Uncertainty: Heuristics and Biases*
Philip Zimbardo's *The Lucifer Effect*

SCIENCE

Rachel Carson's *Silent Spring*
William Cronon's *Nature's Metropolis: Chicago And The Great West*
Alfred W. Crosby's *The Columbian Exchange*
Charles Darwin's *On the Origin of Species*
Richard Dawkin's *The Selfish Gene*
Thomas Kuhn's *The Structure of Scientific Revolutions*
Geoffrey Parker's *Global Crisis: War, Climate Change and Catastrophe in the Seventeenth Century*
Mathis Wackernagel & William Rees's *Our Ecological Footprint*

SOCIOLOGY

Michelle Alexander's *The New Jim Crow: Mass Incarceration in the Age of Colorblindness*
Gordon Allport's *The Nature of Prejudice*
Albert Bandura's *Aggression: A Social Learning Analysis*
Hanna Batatu's *The Old Social Classes And The Revolutionary Movements Of Iraq*
Ha-Joon Chang's *Kicking Away the Ladder*
W. E. B. Du Bois's *The Souls of Black Folk*
Émile Durkheim's *On Suicide*
Frantz Fanon's *Black Skin, White Masks*
Frantz Fanon's *The Wretched of the Earth*
Eric Foner's *Reconstruction: America's Unfinished Revolution, 1863-1877*
Eugene Genovese's *Roll, Jordan, Roll: The World the Slaves Made*
Jack Goldstone's *Revolution and Rebellion in the Early Modern World*
Antonio Gramsci's *The Prison Notebooks*
Richard Herrnstein & Charles A Murray's *The Bell Curve: Intelligence and Class Structure in American Life*
Eric Hoffer's *The True Believer: Thoughts on the Nature of Mass Movements*
Jane Jacobs's *The Death and Life of Great American Cities*
Robert Lucas's *Why Doesn't Capital Flow from Rich to Poor Countries?*
Jay Macleod's *Ain't No Makin' It: Aspirations and Attainment in a Low Income Neighborhood*
Elaine May's *Homeward Bound: American Families in the Cold War Era*
Douglas McGregor's *The Human Side of Enterprise*
C. Wright Mills's *The Sociological Imagination*

The Macat Library By Discipline

Thomas Piketty's *Capital in the Twenty-First Century*
Robert D. Putman's *Bowling Alone*
David Riesman's *The Lonely Crowd: A Study of the Changing American Character*
Edward Said's *Orientalism*
Joan Wallach Scott's *Gender and the Politics of History*
Theda Skocpol's *States and Social Revolutions*
Max Weber's *The Protestant Ethic and the Spirit of Capitalism*

THEOLOGY

Augustine's *Confessions*
Benedict's *Rule of St Benedict*
Gustavo Gutiérrez's *A Theology of Liberation*
Carole Hillenbrand's *The Crusades: Islamic Perspectives*
David Hume's *Dialogues Concerning Natural Religion*
Immanuel Kant's *Religion within the Boundaries of Mere Reason*
Ernst Kantorowicz's *The King's Two Bodies: A Study in Medieval Political Theology*
Søren Kierkegaard's *The Sickness Unto Death*
C. S. Lewis's *The Abolition of Man*
Saba Mahmood's *The Politics of Piety: The Islamic Revival and the Feminist Subject*
Baruch Spinoza's *Ethics*
Keith Thomas's *Religion and the Decline of Magic*

COMING SOON

Chris Argyris's *The Individual and the Organisation*
Seyla Benhabib's *The Rights of Others*
Walter Benjamin's *The Work Of Art in the Age of Mechanical Reproduction*
John Berger's *Ways of Seeing*
Pierre Bourdieu's *Outline of a Theory of Practice*
Mary Douglas's *Purity and Danger*
Roland Dworkin's *Taking Rights Seriously*
James G. March's *Exploration and Exploitation in Organisational Learning*
Ikujiro Nonaka's *A Dynamic Theory of Organizational Knowledge Creation*
Griselda Pollock's *Vision and Difference*
Amartya Sen's *Inequality Re-Examined*
Susan Sontag's *On Photography*
Yasser Tabbaa's *The Transformation of Islamic Art*
Ludwig von Mises's *Theory of Money and Credit*

Macat Disciplines

Access the greatest ideas and thinkers across entire disciplines, including

FEMINISM, GENDER AND QUEER STUDIES

Simone De Beauvoir's
The Second Sex

Michel Foucault's
History of Sexuality

Betty Friedan's
The Feminine Mystique

Saba Mahmood's
The Politics of Piety: The Islamic Revival and the Feminist Subject

Joan Wallach Scott's
Gender and the Politics of History

Mary Wollstonecraft's
A Vindication of the Rights of Woman

Virginia Woolf's
A Room of One's Own

Judith Butler's
Gender Trouble

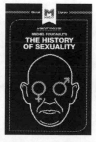

Macat analyses are available from all good bookshops and libraries.

Access hundreds of analyses through one, multimedia tool.
Join free for one month **library.macat.com**

Macat Disciplines

Access the greatest ideas and thinkers across entire disciplines, including

INEQUALITY

Ha-Joon Chang's, *Kicking Away the Ladder*
David Graeber's, *Debt: The First 5000 Years*
Robert E. Lucas's, *Why Doesn't Capital Flow from Rich To Poor Countries?*
Thomas Piketty's, *Capital in the Twenty-First Century*
Amartya Sen's, *Inequality Re-Examined*
Mahbub Ul Haq's, *Reflections on Human Development*

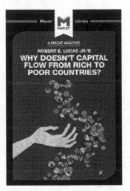

Printed in the United States
by Baker & Taylor Publisher Services